HISTORIC FORT YORK

1793–1993

Fort York
is a historic site museum operated by
the Toronto Historical Board

The Toronto Historical Board was established by the
Corporation of the City of Toronto
in 1960

Fort York is located in downtown Toronto
on Garrison Road off Fleet Street
between Bathurst Street and Strachan Avenue

HISTORIC FORT YORK

1793–1993

CARL BENN

NATURAL HERITAGE / NATURAL HISTORY INC.

This book is dedicated
to the memory of the late
Colonel Charles P. Stacey,
one of Canada's foremost historians and
First Honorary Curator of Fort York.

Historic Fort York, 1793–1993
by Carl Benn

Published by Natural Heritage/Natural History Inc.
P.O. Box 95, Station "O", Toronto, Ontario M4A 2M8

MAPS: Kevin Hebib
COPY EDITING: Wendy Thomas
DESIGN AND TYPESETTING: Robin Brass Studio
Printed and bound in Canada by Hignell Printing Limited,
Winnipeg, Manitoba

Canadian Cataloguing in Publication Data

Benn, Carl, 1953–
Historic Fort York, 1793–1993

Includes bibliographical references and index.
ISBN 0-920474-79-9

1. Fort York (Toronto, Ont.) – History.
2. Fortification – Ontario – Toronto – History.
3. Canada – History, Military.
4. Historic sites – Ontario – Toronto.
I. Title.

FC3097.8.F67B46 1993 971.3'541 C93-094175-6
F1059.5.T688F67 1993

Natural Heritage/Natural History Inc. gratefully acknowledges the assistance of the Canada Council, the Ontario Arts Council, and the Government of Ontario through the Ministry of Culture, Tourism and Recreation.

FOREWORD

by

THE HONOURABLE HENRY N. R. JACKMAN,

LIEUTENANT-GOVERNOR OF ONTARIO

Two hundred years ago Lieutenant-Governor John Graves Simcoe founded Toronto when he established Fort York. Immediately afterwards, he moved the provincial capital from the border town of Niagara to Toronto as a "temporary" emergency measure. Both acts were part of Governor Simcoe's preparations to defend Upper Canada (now Ontario) from an expected American invasion. Civilian settlement followed the government, and a community, named "York," began to grow just east of the garrison.

While the threat of hostilities passed by 1794, ongoing tensions with the United States led to war in 1812. Between 1812 and 1814, British troops, Canadian militia, and Aboriginal warriors marched from Fort York to preserve our sovereignty against foreign assault. In 1813 and 1814, Fort York itself came under attack when American forces targeted the provincial capital in their efforts to annex Canada. Although the Americans captured York twice in 1813 and enjoyed military success elsewhere, the colony's defenders ultimately succeeded in defending our territorial integrity from conquest.

After the War of 1812, British and Canadian troops continued to garrison Fort York to guard the province from foreign expansion and internal unrest. These soldiers and their families made important contributions to colonial society as it grew in size and sophistication. In 1834, this growth saw York incorporate as the City of Toronto, a prosperous centre with a population of 9,000. In 1867, when Toronto had 50,000 people, Canadian society had matured to the point where the British Parliament made Canada a self-governing Dominion.

Often, we overlook the roles the military played in protecting our sovereignty during the formative years of Canada's evolution from colony to nation. Had it not been for the soldiers in garrisons such as Fort York, Canada's distinctive social and national development might very well have been stillborn at some distant point in our past.

As John Graves Simcoe's modern-day successor, I take pleasure in commending this book to your attention. Through it, I invite you to explore the exciting world of our turbulent military past. At the same time, I hope you will spare a thought for the people – most of them now nameless – who defended our society in its fragile formative decades.

THE HONOURABLE HENRY N. R. JACKMAN,
LIEUTENANT-GOVERNOR OF ONTARIO

CONTENTS

LIST OF PLATES

LIST OF MAPS

ABBREVIATIONS FOR COMMONLY CITED SOURCES

AO Archives of Ontario, Toronto
CTA City of Toronto Archives
MTL Metropolitan Toronto Library
NAC National Archives of Canada, Ottawa
NYHS New-York Historical Society, New York City
THB Toronto Historical Board

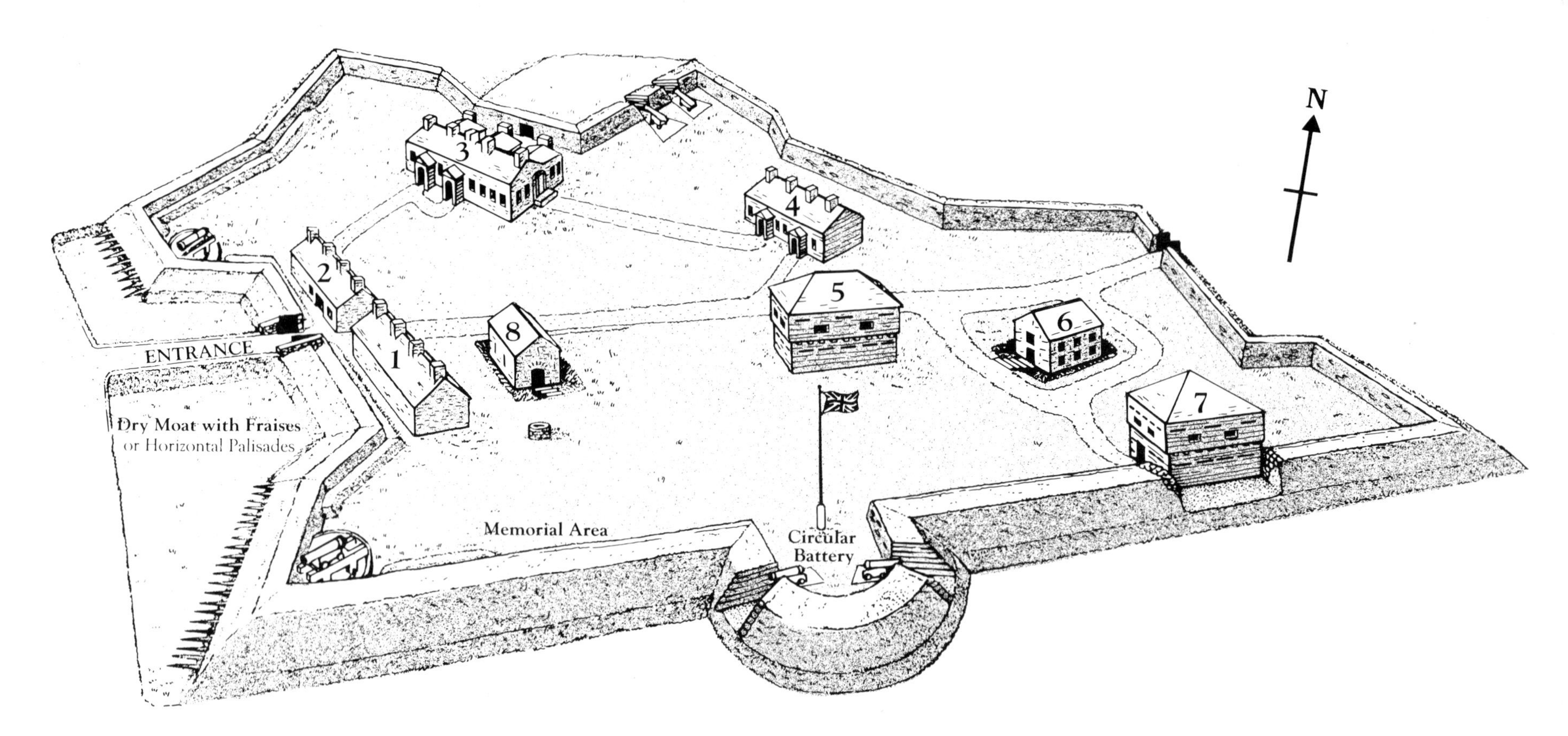

Map 1: Fort York Today

1 & 2 The BRICK BARRACKS, constructed in 1815, each contained three rooms which housed 25-35 soldiers, soldiers' wives and children. By the 1860s, when barracks facilities were improved, some rooms were converted into married quarters with two or three families per room, while others were made into sergeants' quarters, and another room became a school.

3 The brick OFFICERS' BARRACKS AND MESS ROOM was built in 1815 and enlarged in 1826. It was divided into three sections: two served as officers' quarters and the other was the general mess dining room for all the officers in the fort. Married officers usually lived in York (Toronto). There are two money vaults in the cellar, installed in 1838 to store government and Bank of Upper Canada funds during the tensions that followed the Rebellion of 1837.

4 The junior OFFICERS' BARRACKS was constructed in the 1930s to represent an earlier 19th-century building. Much of the present building contains material from the earlier structure.

5 BLOCKHOUSE NUMBER 2, built in 1813, doubled as a 160-person barracks and fortification. The structure is splinter- and bullet-proof, and has musket loopholes and artillery ports.

6 The BRICK MAGAZINE, built in 1814, originally was a bomb-proof gunpowder magazine. However, its walls were unable to support the weight of the vaulted bomb-proof roof and in 1824 the roof was removed and a second floor was added. It then was used as a storehouse for weapons and other equipment.

7 BLOCKHOUSE NUMBER 1, constructed in 1813, could accommodate 124 people. It originally had a cellar that could serve as a magazine.

8 The STONE POWDER MAGAZINE was built in 1815 to provide bomb-proof storage for 900 barrels of gunpowder (each weighing about 41 kg). It has walls 2.2 m thick, a vaulted roof, spark-proof copper and brass fixtures, and a simple but effective ventilation system to keep the powder dry.

PREFACE

The founding of modern urban Toronto was a military event that occurred when John Graves Simcoe ordered the construction of a garrison on the present site of Fort York in 1793. Because of a war scare with the United States, Simcoe wanted to establish a naval base at Toronto in order to control Lake Ontario. In his capacity as lieutenant-governor of the British colony of Upper Canada, Simcoe also moved the provincial capital to Toronto from the vulnerable border town of Niagara during that tense period. Toronto was renamed "York," civilian settlement followed the government, and a community began to grow east of the garrison. During those early years, Fort York played a significant role in the economic and social development of the small backwoods community.

Militarily, the fort saw action in the War of 1812, most notably during the Battle of York in April 1813. After the war, troops garrisoned Fort York to guard the community from threats posed by internal unrest and, more importantly, from possible American attempts to annex Canada. The British army stationed soldiers at the fort almost continuously from 1793 until 1870. After the withdrawal of imperial troops, Canadian forces maintained Fort York's harbour defences until the 1880s when its fortifications and armaments became obsolete. However, the army did not abandon the site at that time, but continued to use the buildings and grounds as an auxiliary facility for the Toronto garrison until the 1930s, and some military activity took place at the fort as late as World War II.

Between 1932 and 1934, the City of Toronto restored Fort York to celebrate the centennial of the incorporation of the city in 1834. On Victoria Day 1934, the governor-general of Canada, the Earl of Bessborough, opened Fort York as a historic site museum. Today, the fort's defensive walls surround Canada's largest collection of original War of 1812 buildings. In addition to their national significance, these seven structures are Toronto's oldest grouping of historic buildings, forming the cornerstone of the city's architectural heritage. Even the one reconstructed building in the fort, the Blue Barracks, contains a significant amount of 1814-period material and is an interesting example of the efforts made during the Great Depression to create employment by restoring and rebuilding historic sites. The grounds of the fort and the land on its west side encompass part of the 1813 battlefield, remnants of Toronto's late eighteenth-century landscape, and a military cemetery. Below the ground of the fort lies a vast archaeological resource capable of significantly expanding our understanding of life in the earliest years of Toronto's settlement.

Today, the City of Toronto, through the Toronto Historical Board, operates Fort York as a historic site museum. The fort houses various exhibits, such as restored period rooms and traditional museum galleries, as well as other displays that tell the story of Ontario's turbulent military past. THB staff engage in the essential tasks common to operating any such institution: enhancing the collection through acquiring artifacts, conserving the collection for the benefit of future generations, developing the site to meet the public's interest in the fort, studying Fort York's history through archival and archaeological research, and sharing that history with as many people as possible through public programmes, tours, and special events. Every year, tens of thousands of people visit Fort York to understand and enjoy the important heritage preserved at the site. A large proportion of these visitors are Toronto-area schoolchildren who participate in the fort's extensive range of educational services.

Surprisingly, despite Fort York's historical importance, a general history of the site had not been produced until I undertook to write this book. My objective in the first three chapters is to narrate the story of Fort York and its place in the broader military history of the Great Lakes region. In the last chapter, my focus changes to recount how Fort York developed as a historic site between the 1880s and the present. My purpose is to provide a readily accessible study so that people can appreciate the fort's story within their larger understanding of the history of Canada.

I am indebted to a number of people who helped in the preparation of this book. Aldona Sendzikas, formerly the fort's assistant curator, spent many long hours tracking down illustrations, helping with research, and supplying other assistance. Within the staff of the Toronto Historical Board, R. Scott James, George Waters, Ian Vincent, John Summers, Cheryl Hart, Susan Kohler, Karen Black, Catherine Webb, David Spittal, René Malagon, David Juliusson, Stan Davies, and Bill Nesbitt (now of Dundurn Castle) contributed helpful comments to improve the text and see the work through to publication.

To Doug Fyfe, Scott Woodland, Christine Lupton, Ray Putt, Tim Dubé, Chris Raible, Stephen Otto, Bill Gray, and Ross Egles, I express my gratitude for bringing useful illustrations and information to my attention. An examination of the picture credits throughout this book demonstrates my debt to the institutions that supplied material from their collections.

To Dr. J. Quentin Hughes (now retired from the Liverpool School of Architecture) and Clair Lemoine-Isabeau of the Musée Royal de L'Armée et D'Histoire Militaire in Brussels, I express my appreciation for information on Fort Wellington in Ostend, a fort that army officers proposed as a model for new defences in Toronto in the 1820s. I also would like to express appreciation for the information and ideas shared by Joseph Thatcher of the Bureau of Historic Sites of the New York State Office of Parks, Recreation and Historic Preservation; Brian Dunnigan of the Old Fort Niagara Association; Steven D. Mecredy of Old Fort Henry; William L. Guthman of Guthman Americana; and Dr. G. Michael Pratt of Heidelberg College in Ohio.

I would like to thank the people who contributed to the physical creation of the book. Kevin Hebib did an excellent job in producing three special maps and Wendy Thomas smoothed out the rough edges of my prose with her editorial skills. Robin Brass receives my particular thanks for his splendid work in designing the book.

Finally, I want to express my most sincere thanks to Barry Penhale, the publisher of Natural Heritage Books, for his enthusiasm for the project and his willingness to undertake the risks associated with publishing a history book in the 1990s.

CARL BENN
Historic Fort York
March 1993

A NOTE ABOUT THE NAME "FORT YORK"

Most people today know the historic site at the foot of Bathurst Street in Toronto as "Fort York" and I have used that title throughout the text for the sake of convenience. However, this name was not used extensively until the restoration of the 1930s, although Peter Russell, who administered the province in the late 1790s, used it occasionally.[1] Usually, people referred to Fort York as "the Garrison," "the Garrison at York," or "the Fort at York" until 1841 when it was replaced by the new garrison. Afterwards, it was known as the "Old Fort" to distinguish it from the "New Fort." In 1893, the New Fort became "Stanley Barracks" to honour the retiring governor-general, Lord Stanley of Preston.

By the 1870s, the name "Fort York" began to come back into use for the Old Fort.[2] When the fort became a historic site museum in the 1930s, it was known as "Old Fort York," a name that the Toronto Historical Board modified in the early 1970s to "Historic Fort York."

CHAPTER ONE

THE EARLY YEARS, 1793–1811

FORCES LEADING TO THE ESTABLISHMENT OF FORT YORK

British authorities began to examine Toronto's potential as a possible military or settlement site in the 1780s.[1] No action was taken until 1793 when the threat of an American invasion of Upper Canada (now Ontario) drove Colonel John Graves Simcoe to establish a military post in Toronto. The genesis of the crisis lay in events that had begun to unfold years before in the 1760s in the Ohio Valley.[2]

With the end of the Seven Years' War and the elimination of France as a power in the Great Lakes region in 1763, settlers from the British Atlantic seaboard colonies flooded into Aboriginal territory on the White-Native frontier. The tribespeople (many of whom had supported France during the late war) responded to this assault on their homes and to other grievances through a widespread uprising, known as the Pontiac War. At first, the Natives enjoyed considerable success, capturing the majority of frontier forts and driving most settlers out of their territory. By 1764, however, the revolt collapsed in the face of a British counter-offensive. As this crisis tore through the frontier, British authorities made a major concession to the tribes by drawing a boundary between White and Native territories in the Royal Proclamation of 1763. This border recognized Aboriginal ownership of the territory more or less north and west of the Ohio and Mohawk rivers. By law, White people could not acquire Native land by squatting on it or stealing it, and individuals and colonial governments were prohibited from purchasing Native lands since

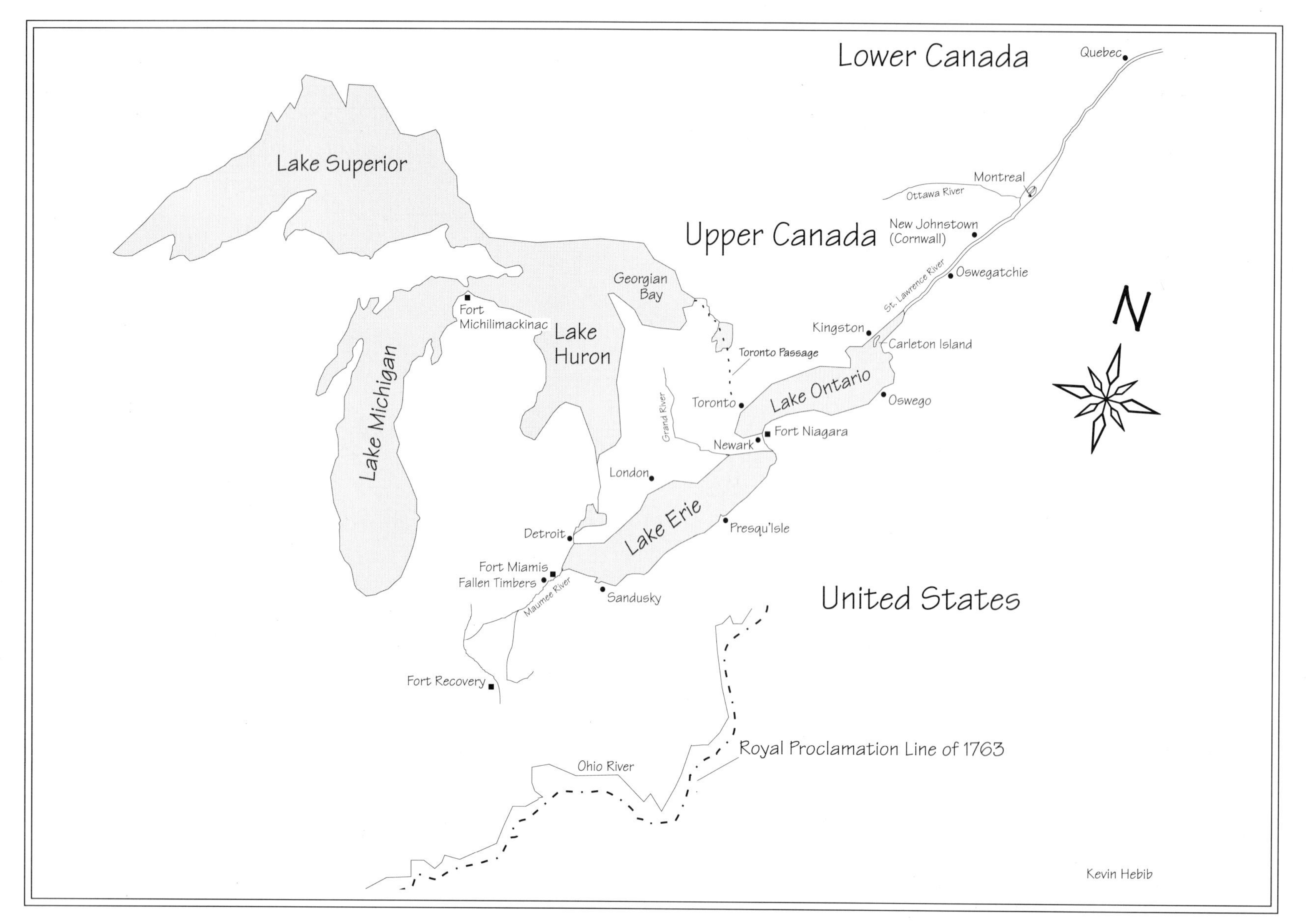

Map 2: The Great Lakes in 1793

such sales usually occurred in exploitive situations. In future, Aboriginal territory could be alienated only by the imperial government purchasing the land from the tribes.

In fact, the Royal Proclamation became a dead letter south of the Great Lakes after thirteen of Britain's colonies declared independence in 1776 and won the subsequent War of the American Revolution with the help of France, Spain, and the Netherlands. The Treaty of Paris of 1783 ended hostilities between Britain and her former colonies and established the Great Lakes as the frontier boundary between the new United States and the remnant of British North America.

This new border held terrifying prospects for the tribes on the American side of the "Old Northwest," as the western Great Lakes region was called. In American eyes, the Natives, as supporters of the losing side in the revolution, had forfeited to the victorious republic rights to their land. To protect their homes, many of the tribes, such as the Shawnees, Wyandots, Delawares, Potawatomis, and Ottawas, waged a guerrilla war against American settlers through the 1780s and into the early 1790s.

The British were implicated in the Native struggle because of their diplomatic support for the tribes and because they violated the Treaty of Paris by holding onto a number of forts within American territory: Oswegatchie, Oswego, Niagara, Presqu'Isle, Sandusky, Detroit, and Michilimackinac. Britain occupied these "Western Posts" in order to stabilize the very tense situation that existed in the Old Northwest immediately following the American Revolution. Many people believed the establishment of the international boundary at the Great Lakes had been unduly generous to the United States because British and Native forces controlled most of the territory north of the Ohio River at the time of the 1783 treaty. For their part, the tribes were bitter about the new border, not understanding why, as the apparent victors in the frontier campaigns of the revolution, they should lose their land to the Americans. As the war ended, British officials feared the Natives might express their outrage by attacking the settlements of United Empire Loyalist refugees on the British side of the new boundary, so the king's forces retained the Western Posts as a forward defence for the loyalist settlements and as a base from which Indian Department agents could work to defuse tensions on the frontier. The British found a justification for violating the Treaty of Paris in the failure of the Americans to fulfil commitments to compensate the loyalists for the losses they had suffered at the hands of the revolutionaries, and in the need for time to liquidate British assets south of the Great Lakes in the immediate post-war period. The Indian Department hoped to engineer a treaty between the Aboriginal peoples and the United States to bring peace to the frontier while ensuring that the Natives would not ally themselves with the Americans against Britain in any future war. The department's agents succeeded in improving Anglo-Native relations by the late 1780s.

Pl. 1: John Graves Simcoe (1752-1806) was the first lieutenant-governor of Upper Canada. Simcoe posed for this painting by Jean Laurent Mosnier in the uniform of the Queen's Rangers in 1791. Simcoe entered the British army in 1770 after receiving his education at Eton and Oxford. He fought throughout the American Revolution and was wounded three times. He gained fame during that war as colonel of the Queen's Rangers, a loyalist regiment noted for its light infantry skills. He married Elizabeth Posthuma Gwillim in 1782. They had eleven children. After the revolution, Simcoe sat in the British parliament before accepting the lieutenant-governorship of Upper Canada in 1791. He arrived in the new province in 1792 but left in 1796 because of poor health. He also served as governor of St. Domingo (now Haiti) for nine months in 1797 but continued sickness forced him to return to England. Appointed commander-in-chief of India in 1806, he became ill on his way there, sailed home, and died in Exeter.

MTL, 1516

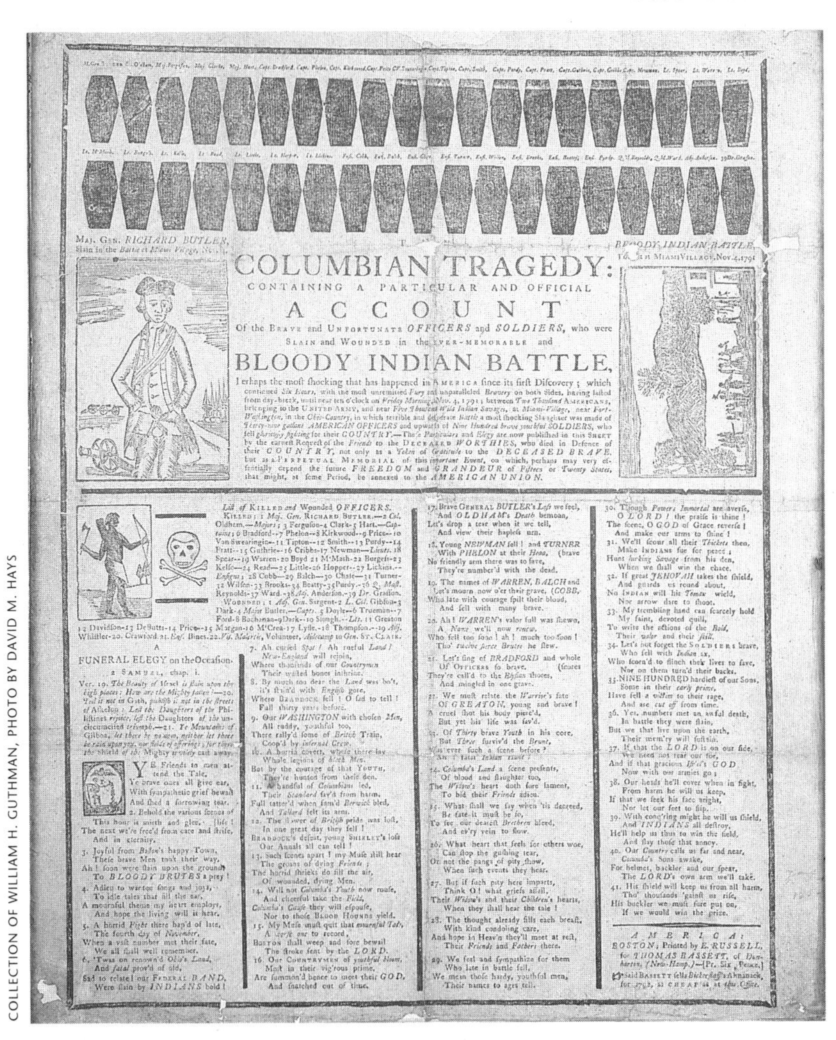

MAJ. GEN. RICHARD BUTLER, Slain in the Battle at Miami Village,

BLOODY INDIAN BATTLE, ... at MIAMI VILLAGE, Nov. 4, 1791.

COLUMBIAN TRAGEDY:
CONTAINING A PARTICULAR AND OFFICIAL
ACCOUNT
Of the BRAVE and UNFORTUNATE OFFICERS and SOLDIERS, who were SLAIN and WOUNDED in the EVER-MEMORABLE and
BLOODY INDIAN BATTLE,

Perhaps the most shocking that has happened in AMERICA since its first Discovery; which continued Six Hours, with the most unremitted Fury and unparalleled Bravery on both sides, having lasted from day-break, until near ten o'clock on Friday Morning, Nov. 4, 1791; between Two Thousand AMERICANS, belonging to the UNITED ARMY, and near Five Thousand Wild Indian Savages, at Miami-Village, near Fort-Washington, in the Ohio-Country, in which terrible and desperate Battle a most shocking Slaughter was made of Thirty-nine gallant AMERICAN OFFICERS and upwards of Nine Hundred brave youthful SOLDIERS, who fell gloriously fighting for their COUNTRY.—These Particulars and Elegy are now published in this SHEET by the earnest Request of the Friends to the DECEASED WORTHIES, who died in Defence of their COUNTRY, not only as a Token of Gratitude to the DECEASED BRAVE, but as a PERPETUAL MEMORIAL of this important Event, on which, perhaps may very essentially depend the future FREEDOM and GRANDEUR of Fifteen or Twenty States, that might, at some Period, be annexed to the AMERICAN UNION.

List of KILLED *and* Wounded OFFICERS.

KILLED; 1 *Maj. Gen.* RICHARD BUTLER.—2 *Col.* Oldham.—*Majors*; 3 Ferguson-4 Clark-5 Hart.—*Captains*; 6 Bradford--7 Phelon--8 Kirkwood--9 Price--10 Von Swearingin--11 Tipton--12 Smith--13 Purdy--14 Pratt--15 Guthrie--16 Cribbs-17 Newman—*Lieuts.* 18 Spear--19 Warren-20 Boyd 21 M'Math-22 Burgess-23 Kelso—24 Read—25 Little-26 Hopper--27 Lickins.--*Ensigns*; 28 Cobb—29 Balch—30 Chase—31 Turner-32 Wilson-33 Brooks-34 Beatty-35 Purdy.-36 *Q. Mast.* Reynolds-37 Ward.-38 *Adj.* Anderson.-39 *Dr.* Grasson.

WOUNDED; 1 *Adj. Gen.* Sargent-2 *L. Col.* Gibson-3 Dark-4 *Major* Butler.—*Capts.* 5 Doyle--6 Trueman--7 Ford-8 Buchanan-9 Dark--10 Slough.--*Lts.* 11 Greaton 12 Davidson-13 DeButts-14 Price--15 Morgan-16 M'Crea-17 Lysle.-18 Thompson.--19 *Adj.* Whistler-20. Crawford 21. *Ens.* Bines. 22. *Vis. Malartie*, Volunteer, *Aidecamp* to *Gen.* ST. CLAIR.

A
FUNERAL ELEGY on the Occasion.
2 SAMUEL, chap. i.

Ver. 19. *The Beauty of Israel is slain upon thy high places: How are the Mighty fallen!*—20. *Tell it not in* Gath, *publish it not in the streets of* Askelon: *Lest the Daughters of the* Philistines *rejoice, lest the* Daughters *of the* uncircumcised *triumph*.—21. *Ye Mountains of* Gilboa, *let there be no dew, neither let there be rain upon you, nor fields of offerings; for there the* shield *of the* Mighty *is vilely* cast away.

YE Friends to men attend the Tale,
Ye brave ones all give ear,
With sympathetic grief bewail
And shed a sorrowing tear.

2. Behold the various scenes of life!
This hour is mirth and glee,
The next we're free'd from care and strife,
And in eternity.

3. Joyful from *Boston*'s happy Town,
These brave Men took their way,
Ah! soon were slain upon the ground
To BLOODY BRUTES a prey!

4. Adieu to wanton songs and joys,
To idle tales that fill the ear,
A mournful theme my heart employs,
And hope the living will it hear.

5. A horrid *Fight* there hap'd of late,
The fourth day of *November*,
When a vast number met their fate,
We all shall well remember.

6. 'Twas on renown'd *Ohio's Land*,
And *fatal* prov'd of old,
Sad to relate! our FEDERAL BAND,
Were slain by INDIANS bold!

7. Ah cursed *Spot!* Ah rueful *Land!*
New-England will rejoin,
Where thousands of our *Countrymen*
Their wasted bones inshrine.

8. By much too dear the *Land* was bo't,
it's stain'd with *English* gore,
Where BRADDOCK fell! O sad to tell!
Full thirty years before.

9. Our WASHINGTON with chosen *Men*,
All ruddy, youthful too,
There rally'd some of *British* Train,
Coop'd by *infernal Crew*.

10. A horrid covert, where there lay
Whole legions of *black Men*.
But by the courage of that YOUTH,
They're hunted from their den.

11. A handful of *Columbians* led,
Their *Standard* sav'd from harm,
Full tatter'd when fam'd *Berwick* bled,
And *Tallard* felt its arm.

12. The flower of *British* pride was lost,
In one great day they fell!
BRADDOCK's defeat, young SHIRLEY's loss
Our Annals all can tell!

13. Such scenes apart! my Muse still hear
The groans of dying *Friends*;
The horrid shrieks do fill the air,
Of wounded, dying Men.

14. Will not *Columbia's Youth* now rouse,
And cheerful take the *Field*,
Columbia's Cause they will espouse,
Nor to those BLOOD HOUNDS yield.

15. My Muse must quit that *mournful Tale*,
A *worse one* to record,
BOSTON shall weep and sore bewail
The stroke sent by the LORD.

16. Our COUNTRYMEN of *youthful bloom*,
Most in their vig'rous prime,
Are summon'd hence to meet their GOD,
And snatched out of time.

17. Brave GENERAL BUTLER's *Loss* we feel,
And OLDHAM's *Death* bemoan,
Let's drop a tear when it we tell,
And view their hapless urn.

18. Young NEWMAN fell! and TURNER brave
With PHELON at their *Head*,
No friendly arm there was to save,
They're number'd with the dead.

19. The names of WARREN, BALCH and COBB,
Let's mourn now o'er their grave,
Who late with courage spilt their blood,
And fell with many brave.

20. Ah! WARREN's valor full was shewn,
A *Name* we'll now *renew*,
Who fell too soon! ah! much too soon!
Tho' *twelve fierce Brutes* he slew.

21. Let's sing of BRADFORD and whole scores
Of OFFICERS so brave,
They're call'd to the *Elysian* shores,
And mingled in one grave.

22. We must relate the *Warrior's* fate
Of GREATON, young and brave!
A cruel shot his body pierc'd,
But yet his life was sav'd.

23. Of *Thirty* brave *Youth* in his core,
But *Three* surviv'd the *Brunt*,
Was ever such a scene before?
An [illegible] *Indian* [illegible]?

24. *Columbia's Land* a scene presents,
Of blood and slaughter too,
The *Widow's* heart doth sore lament,
To bid their *Friends* adieu.

25. What shall we say when 'tis decreed,
Be fate it must be so,
To see our dearest *Brethren* bleed,
And ev'ry vein to flow.

26. What heart that feels for others woe,
Can stop the gushing tear,
Or not the pangs of pity show,
When such events they hear.

27. But if such pity here imparts,
Think O! what griefs assail,
Their *Widow's* and their *Children's* hearts,
When they shall hear the tale!

28. The thought already fills each breast,
With kind condoling care,
And hope in Heav'n they'll meet at rest,
Their *Friends* and *Fathers* there.

29. We feel and sympathize for them
Who late in battle fell,
We mean those hardy, youthful men,
Their names to ages tell.

30. Though *Powers Immortal* are averse,
O LORD! the praise is thine!
The scene, O GOD of Grace reverse!
And make our arms to shine!

31. We'll scour all their *Thickets* then,
Make INDIANS sue for peace;
Hunt *lurking Savage* from his den,
When we shall win the chace.

32. If great JEHOVAH takes the shield,
And guards us round about,
No INDIAN will his *Tomax* wield,
Nor arrow dare to shoot.

33. My trembling hand can scarcely hold
My faint, devoted quill,
To write the actions of the *Bold*,
Their *valor* and their *skill*.

34. Let's not forget the SOLDIERS brave,
Who fell with *Indian* ax,
Who scorn'd to flinch their lives to save,
Nor on them turn'd their backs.

35. NINE HUNDRED hardiest of our Sons,
Some in their *early prime*,
Have fell a *victim* to their rage,
And are *cut off* from time.

36. Yes, numbers met an awful death,
In battle they were slain,
But we that live upon the earth,
Their mem'ry will sustain.

37. If that the LORD is on our side,
We need not fear our foe,
And if that gracious *Israel's* GOD
Now with our armies go;

38. Our heads he'll cover when in fight,
From harm he will us keep,
If that we seek his face aright,
Nor let our feet to slip.

39. With conq'ring might he will us shield,
And INDIANS all destroy,
He'll help us thus to win the field,
And slay those that annoy.

40. Our *Country* calls us far and near,
Columbia's Sons awake,
For helmet, buckler and our spear,
The LORD's own arm we'll take.

41. His shield will keep us from all harm,
Tho' thousands 'gainst us rise,
His buckler we must sure put on,
If we would win the prize.

AMERICA:
BOSTON; Printed by E. RUSSELL, for THOMAS BASSETT, of Dunbarton, (New-Hamp.)—[Pr. Six Pence.]
☞ Said BASSETT sells *Bickerstaff's* Almanack, for 1792, as CHEAP as at *the Office*.

COLLECTION OF WILLIAM H. GUTHMAN, PHOTO BY DAVID M. HAYS

Pl. 2: The greatest Native victory occurred when the allied tribes commanded by the Miami chief, Little Turtle, destroyed the American army in November 1791. This dramatic newspaper account gives a sense of the shock felt in the United States when news of the battle filtered back from the frontier. The Americans suffered over 900 casualties out of 1,400 people present, compared to only sixty Aboriginal losses.

In the United States, however, hostilities between the tribes and American settlers escalated into a war marked by savage brutality on both sides. The climax of Aboriginal resistance occurred in 1790 and 1791 when the tribes inflicted devastating defeats upon two American armies sent to subdue them. The United States responded to these disasters by raising a third army to contest the Ohio Valley. Yet, with the Native demonstration of military strength in 1790 and 1791, many politicians in the American congress wanted the government to negotiate peace with the tribes rather than seek a military solution. Consequently, President George Washington agreed to send emissaries to meet the tribes in council during the summer of 1793 at a British Indian Department station south of Detroit. This effort was doomed to failure. On one hand, Washington and his cabinet were not seriously interested in a diplomatic solution, but agreed to negotiations only because congress would not support a military campaign without a parallel diplomatic effort. Therefore, the American government merely went through the motions of seeking a peaceful settlement.[3] On the other hand, the western tribes came under the influence of hard-line leaders who demanded a boundary that would have been completely unacceptable to the United States even had the government been sincere about a peaceful resolution of the frontier crisis.

With a resumption of the Native-American war in 1793, the British feared the American army would assault the Western

OLD FORT NIAGARA ASSOCIATION

Pl. 3: Fort Niagara was the strongest of the western posts. In the foreground of this *c.*1784 watercolour are vessels of the only naval force on the Great Lakes, the Provincial Marine, which gave the British a significant communications advantage in the region.

Posts or even invade Upper Canada. There was considerable support in the United States for attacks on British positions because many people believed the Natives could not have been as successful had the British not supplied weapons and advisers to the tribes. Furthermore, America's old revolutionary ally, France, went to war with Britain early in 1793 and tried to destabilize British power in North America by encouraging the United States to invade Upper Canada. French agents also tried to undermine the British-Native alliance by telling the tribespeople that their old French allies soon would return to Lower Canada (now Québec) and at the same time attempted to convince French Canadians to overthrow their government. For their part, the Americans supported the efforts of French warships and privateers to harass British shipping on the Atlantic and in the Caribbean in response to British attempts to blockade French West Indian colonies. With American commercial interests offended by the British blockade, Thomas Jefferson expressed American public opinion when he noted that the Anglo-French war in Europe rekindled "all the old spirit of 1776."[4]

THE FOUNDING OF TORONTO AT FORT YORK

With this rapid deterioration of Anglo-American relations, Upper Canada's lieutenant-governor, Colonel John Graves Simcoe, concluded that Detroit was indefensible, Fort Niagara (his strongest position) was too weak to resist the American army, and his naval base in Kingston could be captured without difficulty. He decided to improve the province's defensive position by building a naval base at Toronto to control Lake Ontario.[5] Simcoe thought Toronto was an excellent location from a military perspective. Unlike Kingston, it was removed from the immediate border region and thus was protected from sudden assault. It had a sheltered harbour – the best on the Great Lakes, in his view – with only one entrance, which could be defended easily against a naval attack.*[6]

Colonel Simcoe hoped to link Toronto on an east-west axis to proposed subsidiary fortifications in the province along a network of roads. He believed the roads would provide an alternative to the Great Lakes for transporting troops and supplies in case the Americans won control of the lakes.[7] Simcoe also wanted to exploit a water and portage route between Toronto and Georgian Bay – the Toronto Passage – because he hoped it would allow the British to keep north-south communications open to lakes Huron, Michigan, and Superior if the Americans threatened the Lake Erie-Detroit River route.[8]

Simcoe wanted Toronto to serve as a secure point where

* Today, there are two channels into the harbour, at the east and west ends of the Toronto Islands. In 1793 there was no eastern passage because the islands were a peninsula attached to the mainland.

troops could be concentrated for Upper Canadian defence. From Toronto, British forces could move quickly, in strength, to oppose any American threat. In Simcoe's mind, this strategy was better than the existing policy of leaving small garrisons in the isolated Western Posts where they could be overwhelmed one by one by a large American force. Another weakness associated with these posts was the difficulty of co-ordinating defensive operations with troops scattered throughout the Great Lakes region. Furthermore, he thought removing troops from the Western Posts was desirable because the occupation of American territory served as "an object of Jealousy of the Government of the United States."[9]

In May 1793, Simcoe surveyed the Toronto site. On July 20, 100 men of the Queen's Rangers under the command of Captain Aeneas Shaw sailed from Newark (now Niagara-on-the-Lake) to Toronto by bateaux.[10] When they arrived, probably on the twenty-first, they established a military camp on the site of Fort York by the shore of Lake Ontario. It was this act that was the founding of modern Toronto.* (Today, Fort York is located hundreds of metres north of the shoreline because of efforts to fill in the waterfront south of the fort between the 1850s and the 1920s. In 1793, the site sat on the north shore of the harbour entrance.)

On July 29, the rest of the regiment and a few government officials, as well as Simcoe and his family, sailed from Newark on the *Mississauga*, serenaded by the band of the Queen's Rangers. They arrived in Toronto the next day. The Simcoes set up a tent as their home just to the east of the Fort York site, divided from the military camp by a creek (later to be named Garrison Creek).[11] Simcoe planned to build his main defences on the south side of the harbour entrance at Gibraltar Point (not far from today's Hanlan's Point on the Toronto Island) and a fort with stone barracks for 250 men where Fort York now stands.[12]

The Fort York site had military merit beyond its ability to guard the entrance to Toronto Bay. It also protected the most vulnerable landward approach to the harbour. If the Americans attacked, they probably would sail across Lake Ontario to Toronto, land troops west of the harbour entrance, and then march along the lake shore supported by their naval vessels on the troops' right flank. The fort site was a triangular piece of ground blocking that route. It was naturally defensible against land forces because water surrounded it on two of its three borders: Lake Ontario on the south side and Garrison Creek along the northeast face. Only the relatively narrow western face was vulnerable to an unimpeded land assault but this problem could be remedied with earthworks, palisades, or other defences.

* When Simcoe arrived, there already were a handful of settlers just east and west of Toronto in the areas of the Don and Humber rivers. There is no evidence that these French-Canadian fur traders and United Empire Loyalist farmers either participated in the decision to establish a town or did anything to encourage Simcoe to do so.

MONTREAL MUSEUM OF FINE ART, 1967.1575, GIFT OF G. R. JACKSON AND M. JACKSON.

Pl. 4: British Indian Department officials followed Aboriginal customs associated with meeting in council to maintain diplomatic relations with the tribes. Shown here is a council between British and Aboriginal leaders at Sandusky in 1793 as drawn by Lewis Foy.

MTL, T10333

Pl. 5: Elizabeth Simcoe painted this watercolour of the Queen's Rangers' camp at Fort York on July 30, 1793, about nine days after the founding of the Toronto military post.

On Gibraltar Point, Simcoe wanted to construct a large two-storey blockhouse surrounded by earthworks. He thought the lower floor should be bomb-proof to house a gunpowder magazine and other supplies, and the upper floor should have a strong battery of artillery to command the harbour entrance. In peacetime, the upper storey could be enclosed to serve as barrack space, but be removable during an attack so the guns could be fired. Colonel Simcoe also wanted the upper storey to be designed so that it could be dismantled, shipped, and reassembled at some other point in the colony as a kind of pre-fabricated small fort.[13]

Simcoe planned to establish a civilian community and a naval arsenal and dockyard at the eastern end of Toronto Bay, approximately in the area of today's George, Duke, Parliament, and Front streets. With the war scare, he also moved the provincial capital to Toronto from the exposed border town of Newark; this was meant as a temporary measure until a site he had chosen at London in western Upper Canada could be developed. The province's executive council, similar in function to today's cabinet, held meetings in Toronto as early as September 1793.[14]

On August 27, 1793, Simcoe baptized his little community "York." Ostensibly he chose the name in honour of the Duke of York's victory over the French at the Battle of Famars near the border between France and the Low Countries in May 1793. In reality, Simcoe had decided to call the settlement York before the battle occurred as part of his policy of giving settlements English-sounding names.[15] News of the duke's victory encouraged Simcoe because he believed British military success against France would check American enthusiasm for an invasion of Canada.[16]

Simcoe's grand plans for York were to remain unfulfilled because he could not obtain permission from his superiors to fortify Toronto. The governor-in-chief of all British North America, Guy Carleton, Baron Dorchester, was on leave at the time Simcoe moved to York. Therefore, Simcoe asked the acting governor, Major-General Sir Alured Clarke, for consent to develop York. General Clarke authorized the establishment of Toronto as a civil government measure to safeguard the capital, but would not allow construction of a military post without Dorchester's approval.[17] Upon his return to Canada, Lord Dorchester flatly turned down Simcoe's military request. In Dorchester's mind, there were three things wrong with York. First, the colony's military force was too small to support an additional post. Second, there already was a naval base at Kingston, and Dorchester believed resources should be applied towards maintaining a strong position in the Kingston area to cover the vulnerable St. Lawrence supply route into Upper Canada. Third, Dorchester thought York was too isolated from more established settlements and sources of supply in Lower Canada to be able to meet the requirements of a naval arsenal.[18] (Simcoe himself acknowledged that there probably were no more than fifteen families of settlers between Burlington Bay and the Bay of Quinte, a distance of 200 kilometres.)[19]

Simcoe's main disagreement with Dorchester was over the merits of Kingston, which he thought was vulnerable to attack, especially in winter when the Americans could march across the frozen St. Lawrence River and destroy the post. Simcoe also preferred York because the longer winter in eastern Upper Canada prevented vessels in Kingston from setting sail as early in the spring as they could from York. Finally, York was better placed to stop an American army from the west from threatening eastern Upper Canada.[20] This last argument probably was Simcoe's best. It would have been very difficult to recover Upper Canada through force or diplomacy if the Americans occupied the province unless the British could bring significant pressure to bear on the Americans, either in Upper Canada or on some other front, such as the Atlantic coast. With most of Britain's military resources concentrated against France in 1793, this option likely could not have been pursued.

Overall, Simcoe's strategy was flawed compared to Dorchester's because he did not attach enough importance to keeping communications open along the St. Lawrence River. If the Americans severed this route, it would have been nearly impossible to reinforce or supply Upper Canada. Cut off from the rest of the British Empire, the colony probably would fall. Furthermore, Simcoe's desire to build strong fortifications at York, along with naval bases on Lake Erie and Georgian Bay and an extensive military road network to connect these posts, was simply too ambitious in relation to available government resources and the primitive state of settlement in the backwoods Upper Canada of the 1790s.

Dorchester's disapproval meant that Simcoe could not use military funds to develop Toronto because he could not get York designated as an official army post. As a result, no strong fortifications capable of serving broad strategic objectives could be built. Instead, Simcoe had access only to the more limited funds of the provincial treasury, in his capacity as the civil governor of Upper Canada, to erect barracks with minor defences for the local function of protecting the capital itself.[21]

By November 1793, all that had been built was a sawmill on the Humber River (a few kilometres west of York) to supply Simcoe's needs for lumber, two log barracks at Fort York, and possibly a stockade in case of a Native attack should the United States or France turn some of the tribes against the British.[22] Although discouraged by slow progress in building Fort York, Simcoe took some pleasure in the fact that an expedition from York had demonstrated that the Toronto Passage lived up to its promise as a quick route for supplying the upper lakes.[23] Over the winter and following year, the Queen's Rangers built another twenty-eight log buildings at Fort York, as well as a guardhouse and two blockhouses (primarily intended as storage buildings) at

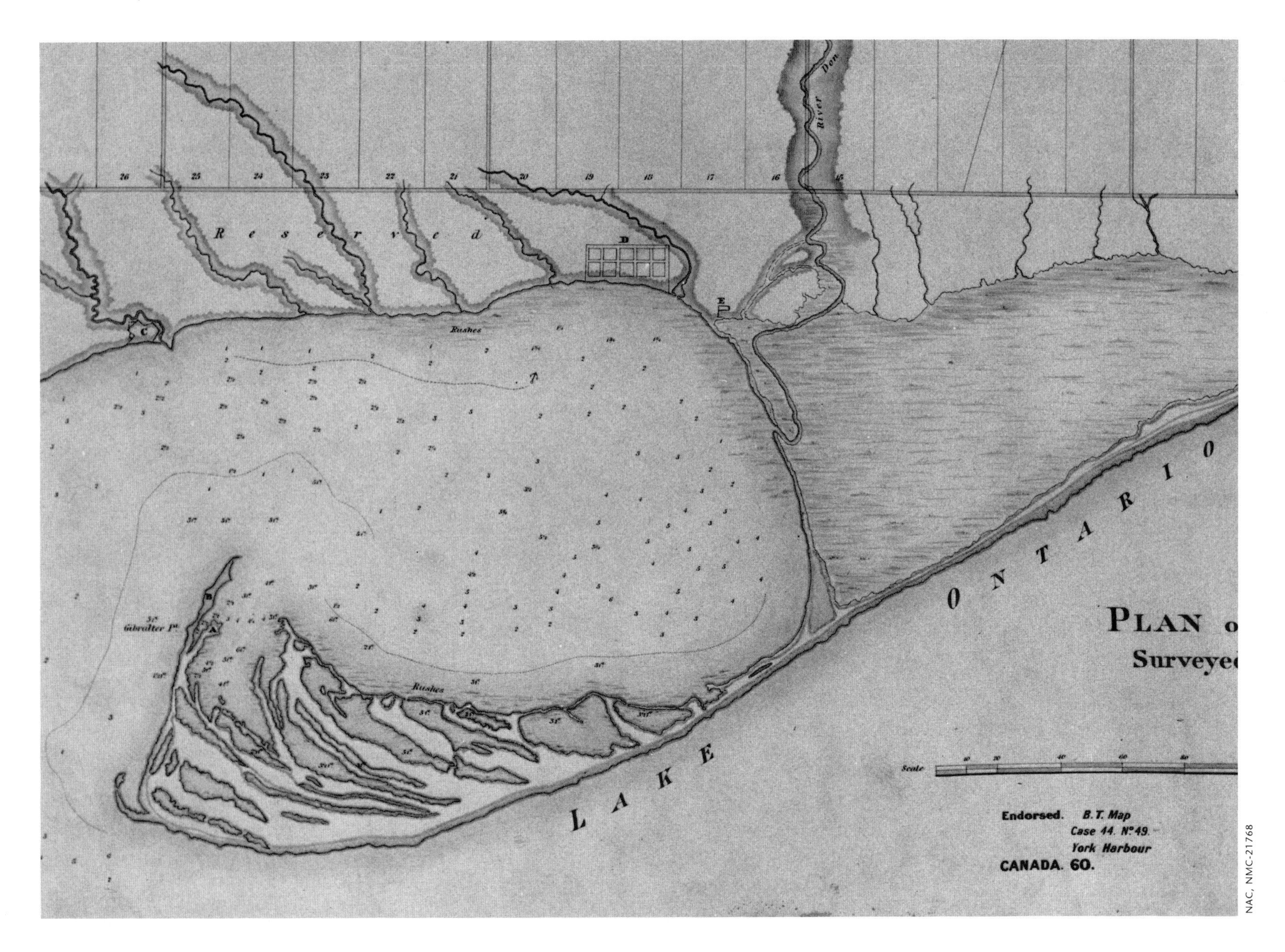

Map 3: "Plan of York Harbour," 1793. The Fort York site is the triangular piece of land between the lake and the creek on the landward side of the harbour entrance at the left side of the map.

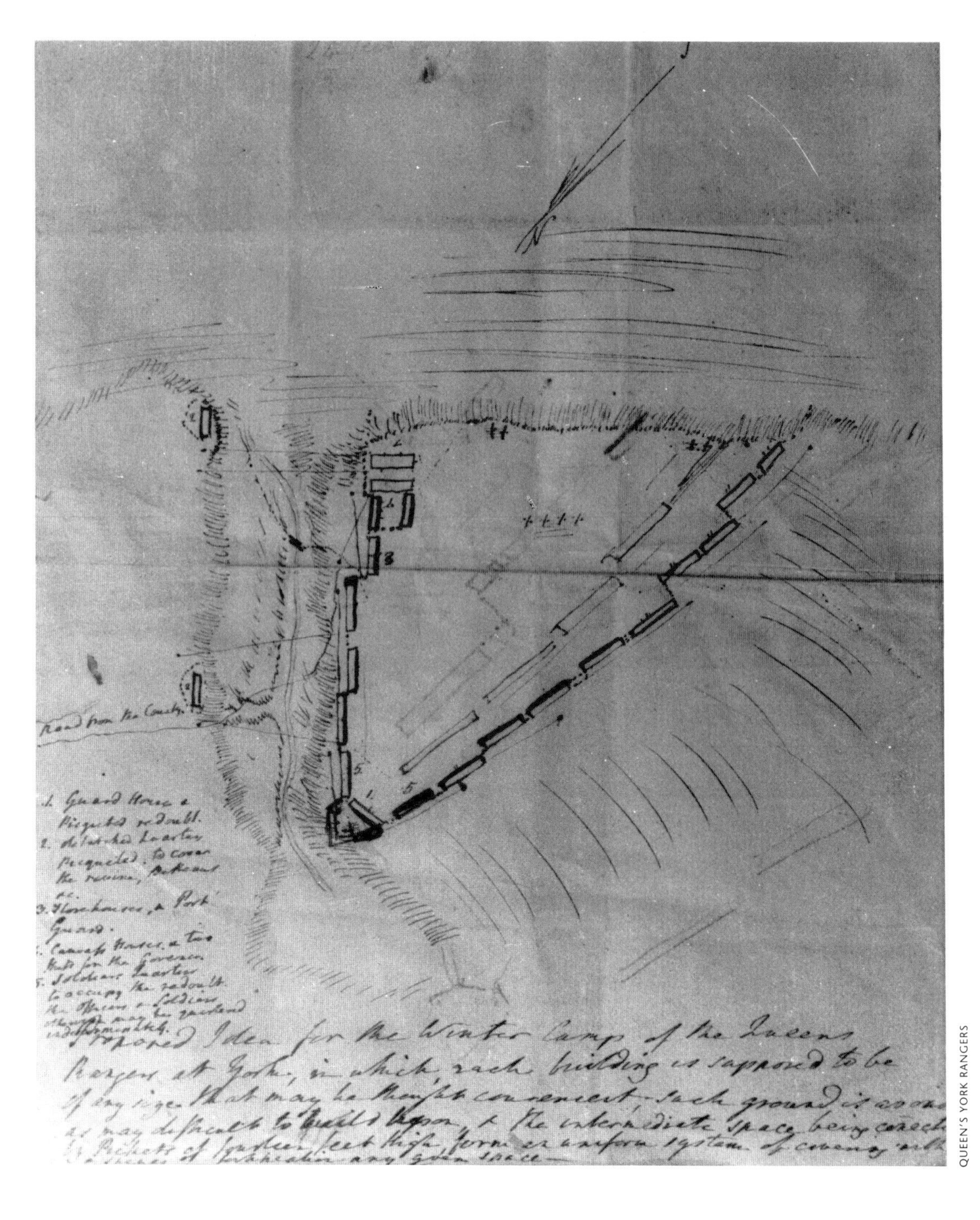

Map 4: Sketch of the proposed winter camp for the Queen's Rangers on the Fort York site, 1793. Note: south (Toronto Harbour) is at the top and north is at the bottom. The scale and geography are distorted.

Gibraltar Point.[24] These latter buildings were more humble than Simcoe's original proposal for the point, but they were nonetheless respectable structures capable of offering strong resistance during an attack, particularly against a force lacking heavy artillery.[25] Simcoe managed to scavenge some artillery for York, including a number of old, condemned guns from Oswegatchie and Carleton Island near Kingston.[26] In the spring of 1794, the Queen's Rangers began construction of Yonge Street, a road designed to improve the Toronto Passage between York and the Holland River, which feeds into Lake Simcoe. To help supply the garrison's food requirements and assist with the development of Yonge Street, Simcoe attracted several hundred settlers, mainly Germans led by William Berczy, to the Markham region northeast of York.[27]

With Dorchester's refusal to build strong defences at York, Simcoe re-assessed Upper Canada's short-term military needs while hoping to develop York when future opportunities allowed. By the spring of 1794, he concluded that humble little York would not be secure enough for the capital in the event of an attack, so he planned to evacuate the government to New Johnstown (now Cornwall) at the east end of the province if the Americans invaded.[28] Realizing that Fort Niagara – the strongest and most centrally located of the Western Posts – would have to serve as his primary defensive position, he began work to strengthen its fortifications.[29]

THE ANGLO-AMERICAN CONFRONTATION OF 1794

As Anglo-American relations deteriorated through the winter of 1793-1794, the American army, under the command of Major-General Anthony Wayne, prepared to march against the tribes assembled south of Detroit. Fearing the worst, Lord Dorchester ordered Simcoe to rebuild a British post from the American Revolution, Fort Miamis on the Maumee River, 100 kilometres south of Detroit, to block Wayne's route to Canada. Re-establishing a base on American territory represented a serious escalation of frontier tension, but Dorchester considered it necessary because he believed war was "inevitable."[30]

Dorchester assumed that the re-occupation of Fort Miamis would send a strong signal to the Aboriginal peoples and guarantee tribal support for the British in the coming conflict by boosting morale among the chiefs and warriors then assembling to protect their homelands against General Wayne. Following the collapse of the 1793 peace council, Dorchester realized that the tribespeople needed to win another major battle to establish an atmosphere of Native strength in which to resume negotiations for a satisfactory treaty for the tribes.

John Graves Simcoe did not want to rebuild Fort Miamis because the Americans would interpret this as a provocation. However, he conceded that the reconstruction of the fort was neces-

NYHS

Pl. 6: Major-General Anthony Wayne (1745-1796) raised a new American army in 1792 to replace the one lost in 1791. By 1794, General Wayne was ready to march against the centre of native power, south of Detroit. If an Anglo-American war broke out, John Graves Simcoe expected to meet General Wayne in battle.

sary because it could stop the Americans from marching on poorly defended Detroit. If Detroit fell, and if General Wayne could acquire bateaux or other vessels, Wayne might be able to sail east across Lake Erie to the Niagara River and conquer the western half of Upper Canada within a matter of days. With the new focus on Fort Miamis, Simcoe moved most of the Queen's Rangers and cannon in good condition from York to the Detroit frontier. Toronto was left with little more than the condemned guns and the invalid soldiers of the Rangers for protection. York's future must have seemed bleak at that point.

At the end of June 1794, the tribes attacked the American supply depot of Fort Recovery, 175 kilometres southwest of Fort Miamis. The garrison's defenders repelled the warriors with some loss. This defeat by a smaller force, combined with serious internal tensions between the tribes, maimed the fragile Aboriginal confederacy and left it gravely weakened when it subsequently mustered to oppose Anthony Wayne's northward advance. In August, the confederacy, supported by some Canadian militia, assembled for the final decisive clash at Fallen Timbers, a few kilometres from Fort Miamis. Conspicuously absent were the regulars from Fort Miamis who had been ordered to avoid an Anglo-American confrontation if at all possible. (The militiamen's presence at Fallen Timbers was "unauthorized," so the British could repudiate their participation if necessary.)

COURTESY OF THE ARTIST AND DR. MICHAEL PRATT

Pl. 7: This modern drawing by Tom Hohl shows Fort Miamis as it appeared at the time of the Battle of Fallen Timbers, based on archaeological excavations conducted by Heidelberg College, Ohio.

The Americans marched into the Native and Canadian ambush. At the sound of the first shots, the garrison at Fort Miamis took up its position behind the fort's defensive walls. Through the trees, the soldiers could hear the shooting intensify as the Americans first reeled, then rallied, and finally drove their outnumbered opponents from the field. Next, the Canadian militia retreated behind the walls of Fort Miamis. The soldiers in the fort then watched the tribesmen pass through the woods near the fort as they escaped from the battle. Later, the famous Mohawk war chief, Joseph Brant (who was not at Fallen Timbers), accused the British of slamming the fort's gates in the tribesmen's faces once the Americans won the battle – a story that is not supported by contemporary accounts of the battle, but that captured the sense of betrayal felt by the tribes towards the British, whose support for the Aboriginal cause was far weaker than the Natives had expected.[31]

The American army, flushed with victory, quickly surrounded Fort Miamis. Several tension-filled days followed. The Americans demanded the surrender of the fort; the British refused. Then, American troops moved close to the fort. The British loaded their cannon. But, moments before the defenders put portfire to fuse, the Americans withdrew. A battle had been avoided by mere minutes. Since the British could not be intimidated into surrendering, General Wayne next wanted to storm Fort Miamis. However, his officers argued that an attack might fail. Even if successful, an assault would cost too many lives because the British were well entrenched and the Americans lacked heavy artillery to breach the earthen ramparts. Diplomatically, the Americans had to avoid a disaster in order to maintain the advantages gained at Fallen Timbers over the western tribes. As General Wayne's supplies were running low and as the majority of his soldiers' terms of enlistment were about to expire, he ended the blockade of Fort Miamis, burned Native crops and a nearby British trading post, and withdrew south a few days after the Battle of Fallen Timbers.

No Anglo-American clash occurred on the Detroit frontier in the following weeks, and British and American diplomats in London negotiated the Treaty of Amity, Commerce, and Navigation (or Jay's Treaty) in 1794. This brought Anglo-American tensions to an end. Defeated, the Native peoples negotiated the Treaty of Greenville with the Americans in 1795; in it they surrendered significant portions of their land (representing much of today's Ohio and part of Indiana along with small parcels of land in Illinois and Michigan). Peace returned to the frontier for a few years, but continued American expansion onto Native territory led to war in 1811 when the Americans launched a pre-emptive strike at Tippecanoe against the western tribes who were engaged in the process of forming a new military alliance.

THE CONSOLIDATION OF YORK

Although the development of Fort York became a low priority in the overall defence of Upper Canada during the crisis on the Maumee River, by 1795 the return of peaceful conditions on the Great Lakes frontier consolidated the fort's position as a home for troops posted to the provincial capital.

In fulfilment of Jay's Treaty, the British turned the Western Posts over to American troops in 1796 and withdrew into Upper Canada, where they built new forts to replace the Western Posts – St. Josephs, Fort Malden, and Fort George. The Americans, in return, made a number of concessions, including a commitment to investigate the failure of state governments to compensate the United Empire Loyalists for the property they had lost during the American Revolution.

AO COPY OF AN ORIGINAL IN THE BRITISH MUSEUM

Pl. 8: "The Garrison at York" from the east by Elizabeth Simcoe, 1796.

Suddenly, though not unexpectedly, Newark, still the unofficial capital of Upper Canada, sat within cannon range of the new American garrison at Fort Niagara. Simcoe began more earnest efforts to transfer the government across the lake to York before retiring to England in August 1796. (His dream of establishing the capital permanently at London seems to have been abandoned by that time.) Peter Russell, who administered the province until the appointment of a new governor, completed the move between 1796 and 1798.

The confirmation of York as the capital brought to the town

increased settlement, which supplemented the slowly growing farming population in the townships surrounding the backwoods community. It would have been inconceivable not to have had at least a small garrison in the provincial capital, so Fort York's future was secured. Nevertheless, in 1796, with the return of peaceful conditions in Upper Canada, the fort was shrunk in size to accommodate a small peacetime garrison of 147 soldiers and their dependants.[32] One positive development occurred in 1796 when the Queen's Rangers finished Yonge Street as far as the Holland River fifty kilometres to the north of the capital.[33] In the next decade, the government opened the Kingston Road and Dundas Street to connect York by land to communities to the east and west.

Simcoe did not achieve his grand plan to make York a strong, fortified naval arsenal on Lake Ontario. Instead, Kingston maintained and then expanded its role as the British naval headquarters for Upper Canada. The only shipbuilding activity that occurred at York in the last years of the eighteenth century was the construction of three gunboats, a bateau, a scow, and, largest of all, the *Toronto*, a small government schooner. These vessels were not built in the harbour where Simcoe had intended the dockyard to be, but on the banks of the Humber River.[34] Accordingly, Fort York's own defensive capability remained modest because the harbour it guarded had little strategic value in the defence of Upper Canada at the close of the eighteenth century.

THE THREAT OF MISSISSAUGA ATTACK

In August 1796, Charles McCuen, a soldier in the Queen's Rangers, in a personal dispute but aided by some civilians, brutally assaulted and mortally wounded the Mississauga chief Wabakinine and his wife on the waterfront at York.[35] These killings aggravated poor British-Native relations caused by another murder of a Mississauga in Kingston in 1792 and heavy-handed government pressure to coerce the tribe to sell much of its land.[36] Over the next two years, the Mississaugas considered attacking the little backwoods capital and the isolated pioneer farms in the neighbouring townships.[37] The colony's authorities tried to appease the Mississaugas by bringing the soldier to trial for murder. Mississauga witnesses, not understanding the nature of European-style justice, stayed away from the trial, and McCuen was acquitted for want of evidence.[38]

Peter Russell took a number of steps to secure York and the rest of the exposed region against attack. The Queen's Rangers garrison available to him at Fort York consisted of only 135 men.[39] To supplement this force, he armed 100 local militiamen and ordered them to hold themselves in readiness to act on short notice.[40] The Indian Department tried to undermine Mississauga military capabilities and deprive them of allies by creating dissension between the tribe and their Iroquois neighbours along the Grand River. The department's agents also attempted to pur-

NAC, C-34334

Pl. 9: "Part of York the Capital of Upper Canada on the Bay of Toronto in Lake Ontario," by Elizabeth Francis Hale, 1804.

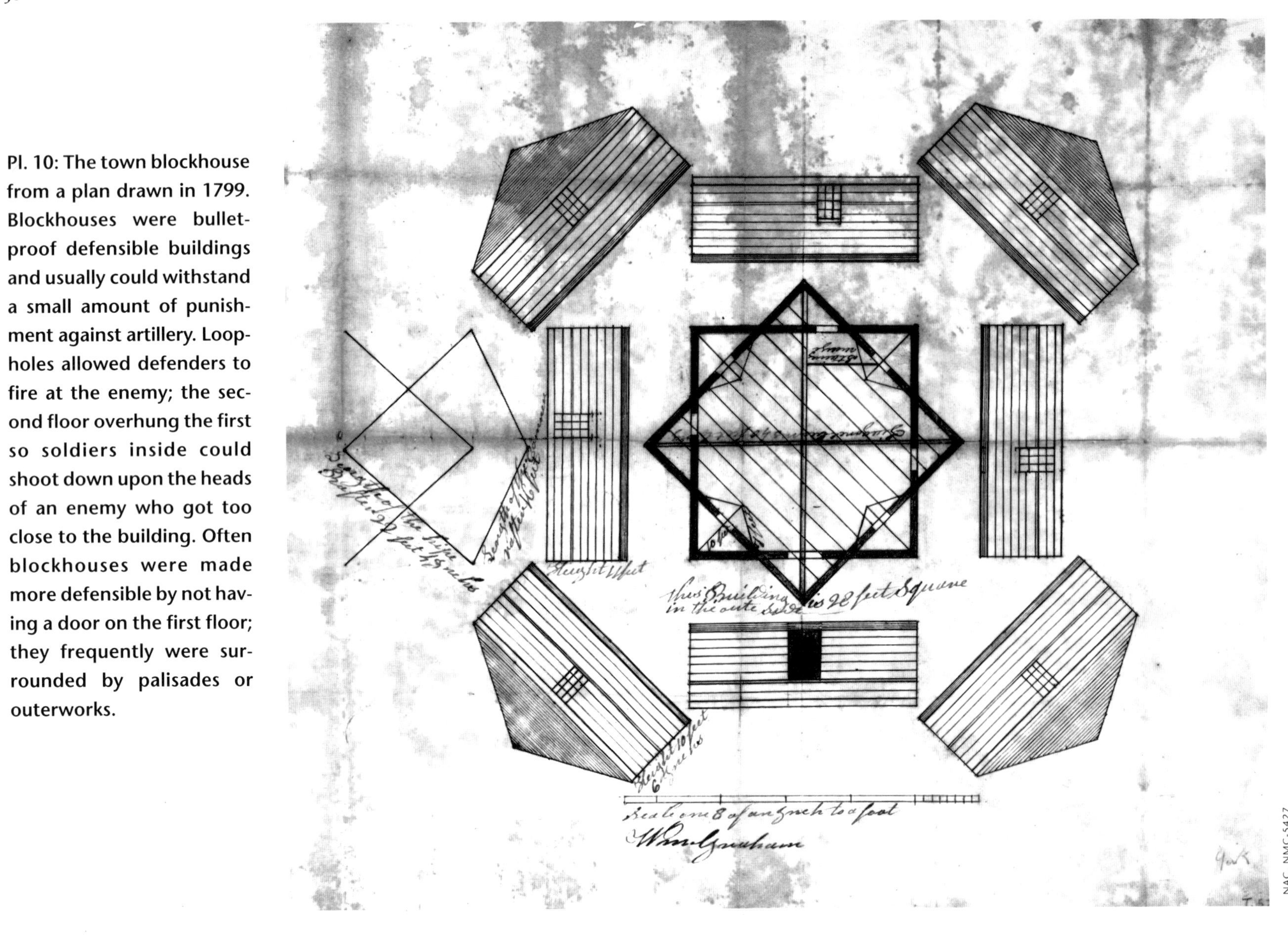

Pl. 10: The town blockhouse from a plan drawn in 1799. Blockhouses were bulletproof defensible buildings and usually could withstand a small amount of punishment against artillery. Loopholes allowed defenders to fire at the enemy; the second floor overhung the first so soldiers inside could shoot down upon the heads of an enemy who got too close to the building. Often blockhouses were made more defensible by not having a door on the first floor; they frequently were surrounded by palisades or outerworks.

NAC, NMC-5427

NATIONAL ARCHIVES OF THE UNITED STATES, RECORDS OF THE OFFICE OF THE CHIEF OF ENGINEERS

Pl. 11: This rare *c.*1799 picture of Fort York decorated a map of Lake Ontario. Visible are the garrison on the left (the current Fort York site) and, on the right, the Mississauga Crisis blockhouse with a signal light on top to guide vessels to York.

NAC, C-14905

Pl. 12: "York Barracks, Lake Ontario, May 13, 1804," by Sempronius Stretton.

chase peace with the Mississaugas through a generous distribution of presents at Fort George.[41]

York continued to suffer under the stigma of not enjoying official army status as a military post during the Mississauga threat. Peter Russell tried to gain access to army funds so he could improve defences by having York designated as a military establishment, but his efforts ended in failure during the crisis.[42] Though willing to maintain the Queen's Rangers' barracks, the army would not undertake any activity to turn the garrison into a proper fort.[43] Nevertheless, Russell managed to have defences improved within the limited resources of the civil budget.[44] He ordered the construction of a blockhouse towards the end of 1797 about 100 metres east of Fort York, near the site where Simcoe had pitched his tent in 1793,[45] but was criticized even for this modest effort. In his defence, he argued that the materials for the blockhouse had been acquired during Simcoe's time and that constructing the building was an economical way of providing new accommodation for the Queen's Rangers because their old barracks, built as temporary structures, had deteriorated badly.[46] Russell augmented the value of the blockhouse by putting a light on its roof to serve as a beacon for vessels entering York harbour.[47] He built another blockhouse early in 1798 in the Town of York for the security of the civilian population and to serve as a guardhouse and rallying point for the local militia.[48]

In the end, a Mississauga uprising did not occur because of efforts made by Joseph Brant from the Grand River to preserve British-Mississauga relations, as well as the Mississaugas' own realization that they could not win an armed conflict because their population was too small to wage a successful war against the growing White population of Upper Canada.[49] Perhaps as a result of the Mississauga crisis, however, Fort York finally was granted status as an official British army post late in 1798.[50]

SIMCOE'S GARRISON REPLACED

By the end of the eighteenth century, most of Simcoe's original buildings, built of green logs and expected to last only seven years, rotted and had to be torn down.[51] They were replaced with new barracks near the 1797 blockhouse (east of both modern Bathurst Street and the present site of Fort York). The new quarters included Peter Russell's blockhouse and nineteen huts, which served as barracks, hospitals, a bake house, and a canteen. Up to 176 people could be accommodated in these buildings while another forty-eight could be housed in the town blockhouse. Other garrison structures included a guardhouse, a gunpowder magazine, a carriage and engine shed, a provision store, and a storehouse shared by the Indian and Commissariat departments.[52] A stockade surrounded the garrison to make it defensible against an enemy, Native or American, who lacked heavy artillery.[53] Most of the huts on the original 1793 site were condemned and demolished. In their place, in 1800, the province built a residence and office – "Government House" – for the new lieutenant-governor, Major-General Peter Hunter.[54]

As the Town of York slowly grew, the garrison functioned not only as Toronto Bay's rather inadequate main fortification, but also as the source of much of the prosperity the local population enjoyed because the army was the primary purchaser of goods and services in the area for the first several decades of York's history. However, prosperity was not constant: in the winter of 1796, government stores from the garrison had to be issued to keep the townspeople alive during a food shortage in the backwoods community.[55]

In 1804, two amateur artists, Sempronius Stretton and Elizabeth Hale, created two interesting watercolours showing York's state eleven years after its founding. Stretton chose the garrison at the mouth of Garrison Creek as his subject. In the foreground are some Mississaugas fishing from their canoes in the lake beside the fort. Up on top of the beach is the garrison: a collection of small wood buildings and Russell's blockhouse. Behind the garrison looms the uncleared forest. Elizabeth Hale painted the civilian town east of the garrison. She shows part of the small community of 430 people clustered on a few streets north of the lakeshore (immediately south of today's Front Street). In the distance, near today's intersection of King and Parliament streets, she painted the brick parliament buildings and the town blockhouse. As with Stretton's drawing, Hale shows the primaeval forest rising up in the background and some Mississaugas in the foreground.

York was very much a modest backwoods settlement largely isolated from the rest of the province. Simcoe, who was living in England in 1804, must have been disappointed that York had grown so little and had played such a modest role in the military affairs of the province up to that point.

CHAPTER TWO

THE WAR OF 1812–1814

THE OUTBREAK OF WAR

In 1807, the captain of the British warship, HMS *Leopard*, ordered his men to fire on the USS *Chesapeake*, thus crippling the American frigate and forcing her captain to strike her colours. Then a boarding party removed from the American ship four sailors believed to be deserters from the Royal Navy. Although the British government repudiated the captain's actions, this incident underscored the growing tensions between the United States and Great Britain.

Britain was in the middle of a desperate war with Napoleonic France. Her strongest weapon was the Royal Navy, which won control over the Atlantic Ocean at the Battle of Trafalgar in 1805. To win the European war, the navy had to blockade France and her allies in order to weaken the enemy economies and prevent vital *matériel* from reaching Napoléon's armies. Despite the blockade, American shipping interests prospered enormously in the first decade of the nineteenth century precisely because of new and expanded markets created by the war in Europe.[1] To keep the blockading warships fully manned, the British rigorously searched out deserters from the navy. Some had joined the crews of American vessels, including United States citizens who had served in the Royal Navy as well as British subjects. A great many Americans strongly opposed the blockade and the navy's searches, regarding them as insults to their national sovereignty. (Historians generally agree that the United States government exaggerated the number of Americans impressed by the Royal Navy. For example, a group of fifty-one New England shipowners knew of only thirty-five cases of impressment over a twelve-year period.)[2] Largely because of the prosperity the European war brought to them, and a relative lack of concern over impressment, the Atlantic states of the American union generally opposed going to war with Great Britain.

The main impetus for hostilities came from people in the western and southern sections of the United States. These people regarded British behaviour on the high seas as an affront to their country's sovereignty, but supported war mainly because of strong regional issues. Southerners wanted to acquire Florida from Spain, then a British ally, and thought war with Britain would lead to the acquisition of the Spanish colony. Westerners coveted the lands of the Native peoples on their borders and regarded the British colonies to the north as natural areas for American expansion. The western tribes, faced with this expansionist threat, began to form a defensive alliance under the Shawnee chief Tecumseh and his prophet brother, Tenskwatawa, in the years before the outbreak of the War of 1812. In the minds of many Americans, defeating the Aboriginal coalition and pushing the tribes off their lands would be easier if the Natives' ally, Britain, could be expelled from Canada. And many people, influenced by strong anti-British sentiments, believed the American Revolution was somehow incomplete because the British had not been expelled from North America in 1783.

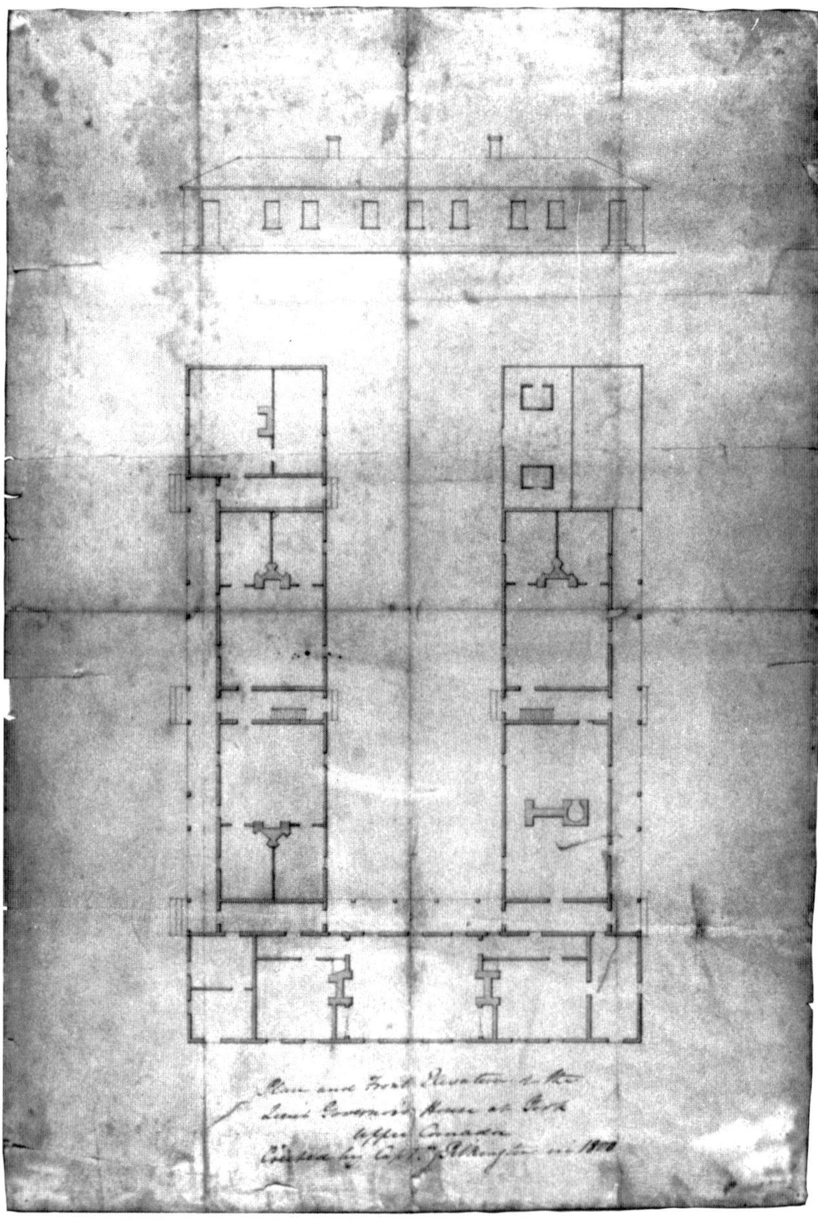

NAC, NMC-5428

Pl. 13: "Plan and Front Elevation of the Lieut. Governor's House at York Upper Canada," 1800.

WILLIAM L. CLEMENTS LIBRARY, UNIVERSITY OF MICHIGAN

Pl. 14: This drawing of Fort York in 1805 shows several important features. On the left (the original fort site of 1793) is Government House. To its right are a few buildings that probably date to 1793 or 1794. The depression beside them is the Garrison Creek valley. On the right is the main garrison, which replaced most of Simcoe's barracks by the turn of the century. Note the 1797 blockhouse and the defensive palisades. ("View of the Garrison at Toronto or York Upper Canada," March 11, 1805, probably by Sempronius Stretton.)

The American president, James Madison, saw significant value in conquering Canada. Before 1812, Madison used economic pressure to try to coerce Britain to change policies the Americans did not like; however, these efforts failed because Britain could acquire most North American products from her own colonies or from American smugglers who used the poorly guarded Canadian border as a way around Madison's trade restrictions. If Madison could conquer British North America, then his country's power would increase immensely as the United States would become the sole source of North American commodities. With such a trade monopoly, the United States could influence international affairs to America's own advantage.[3] By late 1811 and early 1812, President Madison's interest in Canada, combined with the desire for war by westerners and southerners and internal political problems that endangered Madison's Republican party's hold on power, made an invasion of Canada an attractive alternative to previous American policy .

Major-General Isaac Brock commanded the British forces in Upper Canada as the war clouds formed on the horizon. He improved York's defences within the limited resources available to him by building three artillery batteries: one at the site of the main garrison at that time (east of modern Bathurst Street), another near Government House (in the location of today's Circular Battery at Fort York), and a third in the Garrison Creek valley between. The batteries had furnaces to heat cannon balls to red-hot temperatures – "hot shot" – to set enemy ships on fire. To respond to any landing outside the range of these fixed positions, he ordered mobile field carriages for some 12-pounder guns.[4] Brock also constructed the west wall and dry moat of today's fort as well as other defences around the harbour entrance and at the east end of York.[5] The construction of the west wall and the Government House Battery seems to indicate that the current design of today's Fort York – a roughly triangular work to take advantage of the lake front and creek bed that surrounded two of the three sides of the site – had been planned before the outbreak of war even though the army did not complete construction until late in the conflict.

With the approach of war, military and government officials renewed the old debate on the relative merits of York and Kingston as naval bases. Kingston was better situated to control the St. Lawrence River, but York was a more secure location to guard against a surprise or winter attack.[6] This time, however, the argument favoured York. Increased settlement in and around the capital since the 1790s led some military planners to believe the necessary supplies and labour for shipbuilding could be obtained locally. Strategists also thought York was a good site for a naval base because the commander-in-chief of Upper Canada normally lived in the capital; therefore, he could keep a professional eye on the dockyard's operations if it too was located in the town.[7]

The main problem with York was that it was not fortified well enough to protect a major naval base. To remedy this problem, Lieutenant-Colonel Ralph Bruyères of the Royal Engineers suggested that a "strong regular fort" be built to guard the harbour entrance. With secure defences, York could also serve as a rallying point if the Americans overran part of the province and could be used as a secure winter station as Simcoe had suggested back in 1793.[8] Bruyères considered the space occupied by Government House and its battery to be too small for his proposed fort. Consequently, he suggested that it be built farther east, between the existing garrison and the town. The governor-in-chief, Sir George Prevost, however, decided that the best place for the new fort was the old Simcoe site, and surveying accordingly began at the Government House location.[9] Prevost probably thought the Simcoe site was better situated to keep enemy warships out of the harbour because of its location at the entrance to Toronto Bay.

Because the vast bulk of the province's dockyard and other naval resources were in Kingston, Prevost decided to move the naval establishment to York gradually as the capital's capacity to house and defend naval facilities improved and as Kingston's dockyards fell into decay.[10] Beyond this plan, there was an immediate need to expand shipbuilding with the approach of war, so in January 1812, Prevost ordered the construction of a sixteen-gun, 128-tonne schooner, the *Prince Regent** at York, which the shipbuilder finished in June.[11] However, international relations deteriorated too quickly to move the dockyard to York before hostilities commenced. York, therefore, ultimately played only a secondary role in the naval defence of Upper Canada.

On June 18, 1812, the United States declared war on Great Britain. The situation looked bleak for the British. Only 1,600 soldiers were stationed in Upper Canada, and with most of Britain's army tied down in Europe fighting Napoléon, few reinforcements could be sent to North America. In those dark early days of the war, probably most Upper Canadians would have agreed with the American statesman, Thomas Jefferson, when he declared, "The acquisition of Canada . . . as far as the neighborhood of Quebec will be a mere matter of marching."[12] However, the British enjoyed advantages in having a better trained and better led force than the Americans and probably could expect large numbers of Aboriginal peoples to join them if the king's forces enjoyed military success in the early stages of the war.

In July, the American army invaded Upper Canada at Sandwich (now Windsor). Fortunately for Canadian defence, the Americans withdrew to Detroit when they found their supply lines threatened by western tribesmen under Tecumseh and heard that the British had captured the key northwest post of Fort Mackinac. The fall of Mackinac was doubly important because not only did it give the British control over the far northwest, but it led hundreds of northern tribespeople from the lakes Huron, Michigan, and Superior regions to side with the British.

Major-General Brock then took the offensive and bluffed the Americans into surrendering their entire northwestern army, as well as Detroit and the Michigan territory in August. (Brock received a knighthood for this victory.) Farther west, a Potawatomi force destroyed the American garrison at Fort Dearborn (now Chicago) as it tried to abandon that isolated post. In October, British regulars, Canadian militia, and Iroquois warriors devastated American forces in the Battle of Queenston Heights, although the British lost an excellent commander when Sir Isaac Brock was mortally wounded early in

* The navy renamed the *Prince Regent* the *General Beresford* in 1813 and renamed it again in 1814 as the *Netley*. This vessel should not be confused with the much larger *Prince Regent* launched in Kingston in 1814.

SAMUEL E. WEIR COLLECTION AND LIBRARY OF ART, QUEENSTON

Pl. 15: James B. Dennis, who fought in the Battle of Queenston Heights, painted his impressions of that action, the most famous British victory of the first year of the war.

the action. A subsequent American invasion in the Niagara Peninsula in November and an invasion of Lower Canada failed because of poor generalship. In January 1813, the Americans suffered yet another setback when a large force sent to retake Detroit lost the Battle of Frenchtown.

In Upper Canada, the events of the first year of the war lifted morale among loyal citizens while weakening the position of pro-American elements of the population (composed mainly of recent immigrants from the United States). The people of York participated in the successes of 1812. When news of the outbreak of hostilities reached the town on June 27, the regulars at Fort York and a militia cavalry squad left for the Niagara Peninsula. The flank companies of the local militia moved into the garrison to guard the provincial capital and receive additional training.[13] Shortly afterwards, they joined the regulars on active service and participated in the victories at Detroit and Queenston while the sedentary militia took their place guarding the town.* In September 1812, for example, 150 officers and men of the local militia regiment garrisoned the fort and watched other strategic locations, such as the town blockhouse and the peninsula.[14] The York Militia also moved supplies, assisted in constructing fortifications and military roads, and transported prisoners of war (many of whom were kept on a vessel in the harbour while in York).[15] Militia duty was not universally popular and some people did their best to avoid serving. Many individuals resented being taken away from their civilian occupations, some were frightened of military service, and others did not support the British cause.[16]

* Flank companies in Upper Canadian militia regiments in 1812 were better trained and equipped than the rest of the militia.

Other townspeople served on board the ships and schooners of the naval force on the lakes. The women of the town were a driving force behind the charitable efforts of the Loyal and Patriotic Society to relieve wartime suffering by making clothes for the troops, raising money to help militiamen and their families, and engaging in other patriotic ventures, such as making regimental colours for the local militia.* [17] The war brought prosperity to the town as the army purchased immense quantities of goods from the local population and hired people for wartime enterprises, such as the construction of a thirty-gun frigate, HMS *Sir Isaac Brock*,** at the town dockyard (near today's Union Station).[18]

* The regimental and king's colours of the 3rd Regiment of York Militia, made by the women of the town, survive in the archives of St. James' Cathedral.

** The *Brock* was designed to carry twenty-six 32-pounder carronades and four long 18-pounder guns. Carronades were short guns that took up less space on a warship than regular guns and were deadly at close range, although they could not fire as far as regular guns.

Pl. 16: The American Lake Ontario naval base at Sackett's Harbor, c.1815.

NYHS

YORK BECOMES A TARGET

Over the winter of 1812-1813, the Americans re-assessed their offensive strategy and concluded that cutting Upper Canada off from the rest of the British Empire was the key to victory. This could be done quickly by capturing either Montréal or the British naval squadron at Kingston. Secretary of War John Armstrong ordered Major-General Henry Dearborn to attack Kingston across the frozen St. Lawrence River;[19] however, Dearborn grossly over-estimated Kingston's defences and spent the winter making excuses for not carrying out Armstrong's instructions.[20] Instead, Dearborn wanted to attack weakly held York to capture the *Sir Isaac Brock*, under construction at the dockyard, as well as the *Prince Regent*, wintering in the provincial capital. Dearborn thought the acquisition of these vessels would swing the balance of power on Lake Ontario decisively to the American cause. If the Americans commanded the lake, Upper Canada probably would fall. Dearborn argued that the capture of York should be followed by the conquest of the Niagara Peninsula, after which all American troops on the Canadian front could be united to attack Kingston and Montréal towards the end of 1813.[21]

At first, the American government resisted General Dearborn's ideas. Armstrong thought Dearborn's strategy was ill-considered and would be more costly than the immediate capture of Kingston because the American army would have to fight a campaign of several months' duration to take York, Fort George, and finally Kingston or Montréal. In the end, political considerations overthrew strategic sense and led to the acceptance of Henry Dearborn's plan. In the United States, the defeats of 1812 made the unpopular war even less tolerable. In state elections, New Englanders expressed their unhappiness with America's dismal military performance by electing anti-war Federalists instead of pro-war Republicans to state legislatures. New England's opposition to the war deprived the federal government of access to some of the best state militia regiments in the republic. As the winter passed, it seemed likely that the Federalists would win the gubernatorial election of April 1813 in the front-line state of New York. If that happened, Madison's Republicans in Washington might experience considerable difficulty prosecuting the war against Upper Canada. To reap the political harvest a military success might yield, the government agreed to let Dearborn attack York because the chances of an easy victory were greatest and because of the significant propaganda value to be earned in capturing the capital of Upper Canada. Therefore, Armstrong sent orders to Dearborn to attack York early in April before the New York vote took place;[22] however, a late winter kept the ships of the American Lake Ontario squadron at Sackett's Harbor (at the southeast corner of Lake Ontario) at anchor longer than expected, jeopardizing the political value of the attack. The Republicans overcame this problem by circulating victory proclamations in advance of the battle to an unsuspecting electorate and by spending large sums of money on war-related projects in New York State. Yet the governing Republicans were so nervous about their chances that, for the most part, they held back the New York troops from the expedition against York because the soldiers' votes were desperately needed to prop up the Republican cause.[23]

While the Americans plotted their strategy, the British worried about the fate of York because wartime shortages prevented them from building the strong works necessary to defend the town; for example, early in April Major-General Sir Roger Sheaffe, who succeeded Brock at Queenston Heights as commander-in-chief and administrator of the province, ordered government officials to hide their papers in the forests and fields behind York to ensure that they would not be lost if the Americans captured the capital. Realizing that an attack might succeed, Sheaffe hoped to finish the *Sir Isaac Brock* before the ice cleared at Sackett's Harbor so the frigate, with the *Prince Regent*, could sail to the relative safety of Kingston and avoid capture.[24] Unfortunately, the construction of the *Brock* went much more slowly than expected, partly because of supply problems and partly because of bad relations between the shipbuilder and government officials. The delay led some strategists to believe that York could not be made a naval base until after the war because shortages made it impossible for the town to become "well established" in light of wartime conditions.[25]

THE BATTLE OF YORK

On April 23, 1813, the Americans at last left Sackett's Harbor for York, but went only a short distance when strong winds from the west forced them to return to port and wait for the storm to clear on April 24. These same winds carried the *Prince Regent* from York to Kingston. The *Sir Isaac Brock*, however, still sat unfinished on the stocks.[26] On April 25, the Americans set sail again with fourteen vessels in the squadron, mounting eighty-three guns and manned by 700 officers and ratings and an unknown number of marines.[27] On board was an army brigade of 1,750 officers and men from the 6th, 14th, 15th, 16th, and 21st Regiments of Infantry, a volunteer regiment composed of men from New York City, Albany, and Baltimore, as well as a company of the 1st Rifle Regiment and either two companies of the 3rd Regiment of Artillery or one each of the 3rd and the Regiment of Light Artillery equipped with field guns.[28] Major-General Henry Dearborn exercised overall command of the expedition. Under him, Commodore Isaac Chauncey led the naval squadron, and the land force fell under the leadership of the famous western explorer, Brigadier-General Zebulon Montgomery Pike.

On April 26, 1813, sentries on Scarborough Bluffs and on the Peninsula spotted the American squadron. Using signal guns and a telegraph – a kind of flagpole on which pennants and other objects could be hung to communicate different messages – the guards warned the town and garrison of the imminent danger.[29] Responsibility for the defence of York lay with Sir Roger Sheaffe. The town's main defences were the 1790s blockhouses located in the town, at the garrison, and on Gibraltar Point, as well as the three batteries at the garrison, and another – the Western Battery – located just north of today's Automotive Building in the Canadian National Exhibition grounds. Other defensive works consisted of the fort's west wall and a small unarmed earthwork located approximately where Fort York Armouries now stand between Fort York and the Western Battery. There were a dozen or so cannon mounted at these and other positions in addition to two 6-pounders on field carriages.[30] Some of the guns were Simcoe's old condemned artillery from 1793.

Sheaffe's force consisted of two companies of the 8th Regiment of Foot (a battalion company and the grenadier company), about a company's worth of two fencible regiments (the Glengarry Light Infantry from eastern Upper Canada and the Royal Newfoundland Regiment), thirteen men of the Royal Artillery, a small squad of the 49th Regiment of Foot, and forty or fifty Mississauga and Ojibway chiefs and warriors. Three hundred and fifty York and Durham militiamen, incorporated militiamen, dockyard workers, and naval personnel also were at his disposal. Total British strength from these various units numbered between 700 and 750 officers and men. Somewhere on the Kingston Road east of York marched the light company of the 8th Regiment, which Sheaffe hoped would arrive in time for action.[31]

Sheaffe expected a two-pronged attack. He assumed that the Americans would land west of Fort York and attack in strength under the cover of a naval barrage and attack in the east from Scarborough. Such a plan would compel him to divide his small force to fight on two fronts and cut off his escape route to Kingston should the battle go badly for the British. He decided to concentrate his troops in two positions. The Natives, most of the professional troops, and some of the militia assembled at Fort York to guard the western approach. The battalion company of the 8th Foot and the bulk of the militia took up a position two kilometres east, at the market square and blockhouse in York, to cover the easterly approach.[32]

On the morning of Tuesday, April 27, General Sheaffe watched the American squadron sail west past the Peninsula towards the ruins of old Fort Rouillé, a small French trading post abandoned in 1759, less than two kilometres west of Fort York (near today's bandshell at the western end of the CNE grounds). From intelligence received earlier, Sheaffe knew that no Americans had landed in Scarborough and that there would be no attack from the east. Consequently, he ordered the regulars and militia stationed in the town to march to his aid at Fort York. To stop the Americans from coming ashore, he sent the Glengarries, Mississaugas, and Ojibways to the expected landing site. Sheaffe kept the rest of his force in reserve at the garrison because he was not sure if the Americans really intended to land at Fort Rouillé, or if their movements were only a feint to draw him out of Fort York, so they then could move east and land between Sheaffe and the town and thereby separate him from his main defences.[33]

Three things went wrong for the British as General Sheaffe deployed his troops. First, high winds from the east blew the American landing craft much farther west than anticipated, thus inadvertently placing the American squadron with its heavy guns between the landing site and the British line of march. This meant that Sheaffe's men could not move quickly along the lake road because the American naval artillery would tear them apart. Instead, they had to make their way slowly through the forest back from the lake shore. This problem prevented the troops from getting to the landing site before the Americans started for shore. Second, a militia officer, Major-General Aeneas Shaw, who had been ordered to watch the back road that led into York from the west (where Queen Street is today), directed the Glengarry Light Infantry to his support instead of letting them obey Sheaffe's command to support the Natives. Third, the troops from town did not arrive as quickly as expected, forcing Sheaffe to send his reserves (consisting of the Royal Newfoundland Fencibles, the grenadier company of the 8th Regiment, and some militia in the garrison) west to support the Natives. This deprived Sheaffe of a reserve that he could deploy to meet changing conditions as the battle developed. Because of these problems, only the Mississaugas and Ojibways were in position when the

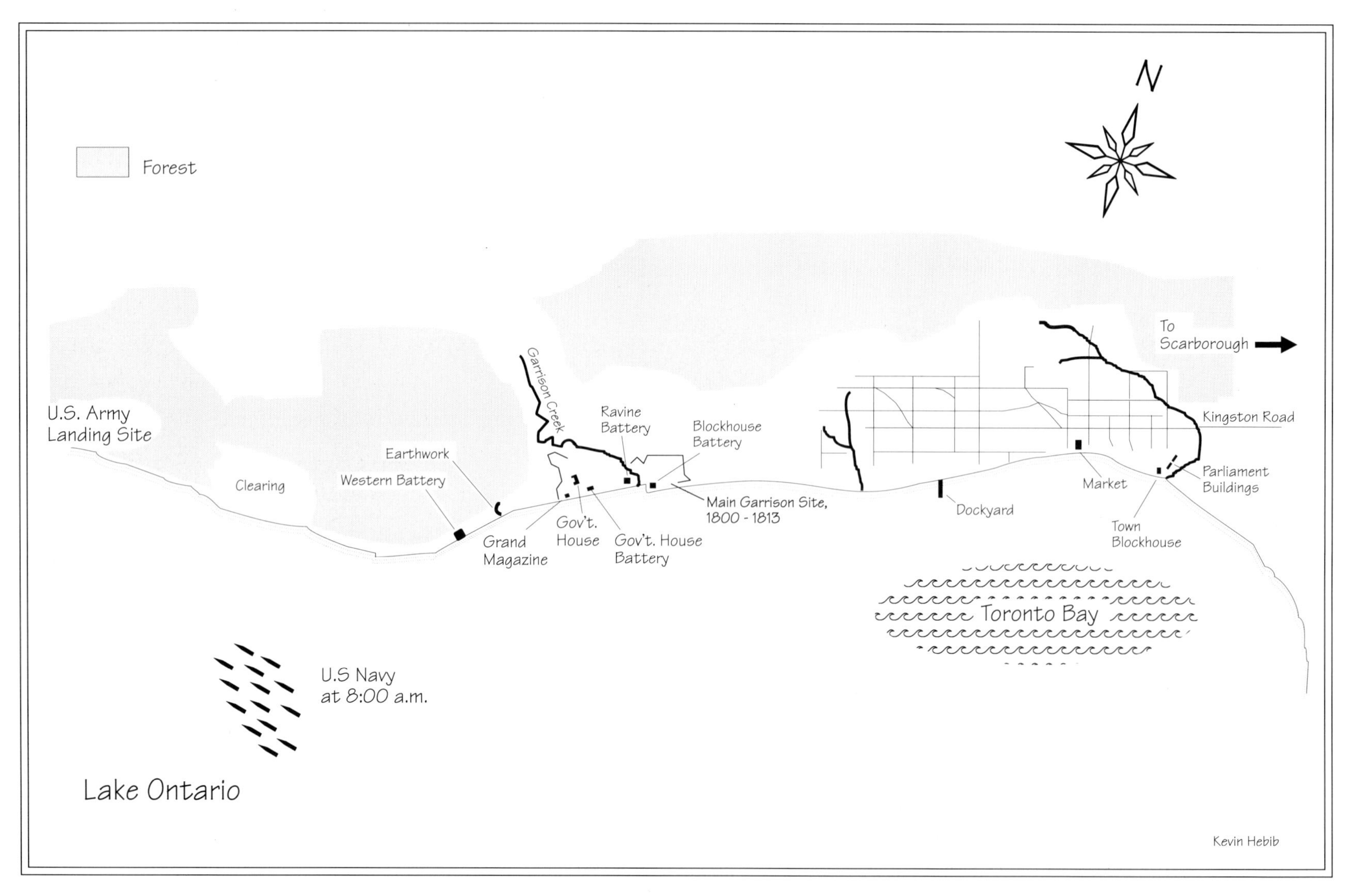

Map 5: The Battle of York, April 27, 1813.

first American boats approached the shoreline at about 8:00 A.M. in what today is Parkdale, near Dowling Avenue, between Dufferin Street and Roncesvalles Avenue.[34]

As the American boats rowed close to the beach, packed with men of the 1st Rifles, the Natives took aim with their muskets and rifles, then let loose a deadly volley into the attackers. The riflemen stopped and ineffectively shot back from their bobbing boats. On board one of the American ships, Brigadier-General Pike watched his men's consternation, apparently exclaimed, "By God, I can't stand here any longer," and led three companies of the 15th Regiment of Infantry towards the beach in support of the riflemen. The 1st Rifles regained their composure, dashed ashore, scrambled up a steep bank, and chased the Natives off into the woods after inflicting eight casualties upon the chiefs and warriors.[35]

Soon afterwards, the grenadier company of the 8th, after trudging through the forest from Fort York, emerged from the bush on top of a bank overlooking the landing site. Although outnumbered three-to-one, they fired a volley and charged into the American ranks. The grenadiers drove the 15th Infantry right off the beach. One grenadier bayonetted an American officer before his enemy even got out of a rowboat. However, the American riflemen, having returned to the waterfront, turned their weapons on the grenadiers while the guns of the American squadron ripped apart the shoreline. With heavy casualties, including the loss of their company commander, the grenadiers withdrew.*[36]

The Americans continued to land in strength. The Glengarry Light Infantry, supported by the remnant of the grenadier company and the Royal Newfoundlanders, then came into action against the Americans. Soon, the battalion company of the 8th Regiment from town joined them in forming a loose thin line to harass both the Americans coming ashore and those already landed.[37] Outnumbered badly and bombarded by the American squadron on their left flank, the British could not stop the enemy from establishing a secure beach head. They found themselves forced to fall back eastward (through today's CNE grounds) with the Americans in pursuit. General Sheaffe twice tried to rally his little force and, at one point, formed them in line and turned back an advancing American column, but his numbers were just too small to be effective, and the Americans continued to push him back.[38]

Sheaffe's main problem was that he was fighting with only half his force. For some unknown reason, the York Militia had not arrived at the battle site despite Sheaffe's orders to march to his aid. There was no physical reason for the militiamen to be

---

* An old Toronto legend claims that the grenadiers retreated westward and met their doom when they fell through the ice on Grenadier Pond in High Park. The story is utter nonsense. The pond got its name as a Victorian romanticism because soldiers from the garrison spent some of their leisure time fishing in its waters.

absent because the battalion company of the 8th Regiment originally posted in the town with the militia had made it to the battlefield some time earlier. Morale was not the problem, either, because the militia had assembled with "the greatest cheerfulness" the night before.[39] The blame rests with their commanding officer, Lieutenant-Colonel William Chewett, but the reason he decided to hold his troops back has never been discovered.

Without Chewett's support, Sheaffe retreated to the Western Battery. The American squadron also moved eastward and brought the battery under heavy fire while the soldiers ashore (with their fifes and drums playing "Yankee Doodle") marched towards the battery.[40] Next, disaster struck at the battery. Somehow, a spark fell into a travelling gunpowder magazine. The subsequent explosion ripped through the Western Battery, knocked over one of the guns, and killed or wounded thirty men. Sheaffe cleared the casualties as quickly as possible and turned the one remaining gun away from the American squadron and aimed it towards the lake road to face the advancing American army. As Zebulon Pike's troops emerged from the woods, the gun opened fire. However, it could not be depressed low enough to inflict much damage because it had been mounted high to shoot out into the lake.[41] The only damages the Americans recorded were broken bayonets and pikes from cannon balls whistling over their heads. (Zebulon Pike had introduced pikes – a kind of spear used as a stabbing weapon – for widespread use into his regiment, the 15th Infantry.)[42]

Sheaffe had no alternative but to retreat to Fort York, where he found Chewett's militiamen finally beginning to form for battle – too late to do any good. The American squadron took up a new position a few hundred metres south of the fort and opened fire. According to one eyewitness, "the Balls came so hott" that soldiers had to lie close under the fort's walls to shield themselves from the barrage.[43] Meanwhile, the American army advanced towards the garrison and halted just west of the fort on what today is Garrison Common. Zebulon Pike brought up a field gun and an artillery duel took place until the garrison guns stopped firing – except for one of Simcoe's condemned guns, an old French 18-pounder located in the Garrison Creek valley; it continued to blast away at the American squadron.[44]

Sheaffe, recognizing that he had lost the battle, ordered his men to withdraw quietly east along Front Street towards the town. At the same time, he (or possibly another senior officer) rode up to and entered Government House for a few minutes, presumably to take or destroy military papers and prevent them from falling into enemy hands.[45] Either by accident or design, the Royal Standard, flown whenever a British fort was under attack in those days, was left up the flagpole, so the Americans, assuming the British still were inside the silent fort, waited for them to come out and surrender. As they waited, a tremendous explosion shook the ground.

Sheaffe had ordered the Grand Magazine (located near to-

COURTESY OF THE PRESENT DUKE OF NORTHUMBERLAND

Pl. 17: Sir Roger Hale Sheaffe (1763-1851), painted by Mather Brown *c.*1787. Born in Boston, Massachusetts, Sheaffe's widowed mother persuaded the Duke of Northumberland (who lodged at her home during the American Revolution) to take an interest in Roger's future. The duke sent Sheaffe to an English military academy and supported his army career, which began with the purchase of an ensign's commission in 1778. Sheaffe saw extensive service in North America as well as in Ireland, Holland, England, and the Baltic. When Isaac Brock died early in the Battle of Queenston Heights, Sheaffe took command of the British forces and inflicted a humiliating defeat upon the Americans. Throughout the winter of 1812-1813, Sheaffe acted as civil administrator of Upper Canada as well as the senior military officer in the province. Replaced in command of Upper Canada after the Battle of York, Sheaffe next served in the Montréal district until recalled to England late in 1813.

day's Memorial Area in the fort) blown up to prevent the gunpowder and munitions stored there from falling into enemy hands.[46] Somewhere along Front Street, P. Finan, the teenage son of the quartermaster of the Royal Newfoundland Regiment, saw the explosion.[47] He recorded: "I . . . felt a tremulous motion in the earth resembling the shock of an earthquake, and looking towards the spot I saw an immense cloud ascend into the air. ... At first it was a great confused mass of smoke, timber, men, earth, &c., but as it rose in a most majestic manner it assumed the shape of a vast balloon."[48] After the debris from the explosion finished its upward ascent, it plunged back to earth with devastating force on the American side. One officer said that the rubble raked the army from front to rear.[49] The blast knocked 250 Americans, dead and wounded, to the ground.[50] Among those mortally wounded was Zebulon Pike, probably "stamped . . . for the Grave" when a rock struck him in the forehead.[51] (Other witnesses said Pike's back was crushed by falling debris.)[52] He died later that day. The blast also inflicted a handful of casualties on the British side among men who failed to get away from the garrison area in time.*

Command of the American forces ashore descended to Colonel Cromwell Pearce, who reorganized his men as quickly as possible because he expected the British to counter-attack.[53] (General Dearborn was not ashore at the time. Instead, he watched the battle from on board the squadron.)[54] Sheaffe, however, was beaten and did not march his men back to the battlefield. The only resistance came from the condemned gun in the creek valley, which continued to fire for a brief period after the explosion.[55]

On the way from the fort to the town, Sheaffe gave orders to burn the *Sir Isaac Brock* and a large quantity of naval supplies to stop them from falling into American hands.[56] Rather than let his valuable professional soldiers and shipwrights become prisoners, he decided to march them to Kingston. Sheaffe left the militia behind to surrender the town. At the east end of the town, Sheaffe met the light company of the 8th Foot, which had just arrived. To slow the Americans should they pursue him (which they did not), Sheaffe burned the Don bridge and deployed the light company to cover his retreat.[57]

Back in the American lines, Colonel Pearce, wondering why he was not attacked, sent skirmishers through the garrison to look for the British. The only people they saw were two who were running away, Lieutenant Ely Playter of the York Militia and the officers' mess cook, a Mrs. Chapman. The Americans opened fire, but Playter and Chapman escaped unharmed.[58] The Ameri-

* The exact number is not known. The evidence suggests that no more than six people were killed or wounded in the explosion on the British side – almost all militia – despite popular accounts to the contrary. Only ten militiamen were killed or wounded in the entire battle. Yet popular accounts suggest that forty militiamen fell in the explosion of the magazine alone.

NAC, C-7434

Pl. 18: The mortal wounding of Zebulon Pike during the explosion of the Grand Magazine from a *c.*1815 print.

UNITED STATES NAVAL ACADEMY MUSEUM, ANNAPOLIS

Pl. 19: At the end of the battle, the Americans captured the Royal Standard that flew over Fort York and used it as a pillow for Zebulon Pike in the hours before he succumbed to his wounds.

cans then advanced through the garrison towards York but had to stop somewhere along Front Street west of today's Spadina Avenue because of dense clouds of smoke blowing in their faces from the burning *Brock*.[59] Next, the Americans saw three figures walking towards them. They were Colonel Chewett, Major William Allan (Chewett's second-in-command), and the Reverend John Strachan, the Church of England rector of York (who, unlike the two militia officers, had been in the thick of the battle evacuating wounded from the Western Battery).[60] These men had come to surrender the capital of Upper Canada.

The Americans were furious. Not only had they just fought a very tough six-hour battle and suffered heavy casualties (totalling 320 Americans compared to 157 British losses),[61] but they quickly realized that there were no warships to capture. To increase their frustration, Sir Roger Sheaffe, the senior general in Upper Canada and head of the civil government, along with his regulars and fencibles, had escaped to fight another day.

With difficulty, Chewett, Allan, and Strachan arranged a capitulation.[62] They agreed to surrender the town, turn over all public stores to the Americans, and surrender any troops in York as prisoners of war (consisting mainly of militiamen and wounded professionals). The militia were to be "paroled," which meant that they could remain at home and not go into a prison camp in the United States, but could not fight again until "exchanged" with captured American troops. The Americans agreed to respect private property, allow civil government authorities to carry out their duties, and permit surgeons to attend to the British wounded.[63]

The American army next continued its march into the town and ordered the members of the York Militia to ground their arms. Most of the Americans and the militia then returned to the garrison where only the militia officers were set free on parole, the rest of the men being locked up under the watchful eyes of American guards.[64]

THE OCCUPATION OF YORK

For some, the occupation of York started off promisingly enough. American troops gave food to the families of British soldiers stranded in York after the retreat of their husbands and fathers. One citizen noted with some astonishment that he saw men conversing with the "greatest familiarity" who only two hours before had been doing their utmost to kill one another.[65] But sadly, the six-day occupation turned out to be an ugly affair for the citizens of York. People experienced the trauma of watching their houses and businesses looted by American rank and file soldiers in contravention of the terms of capitulation. Even some American officers participated in the thievery,[66] while others, ashamed of their men's behaviour, personally stood guard over people's homes.[67] One victim was Angelique Givins, who suf-

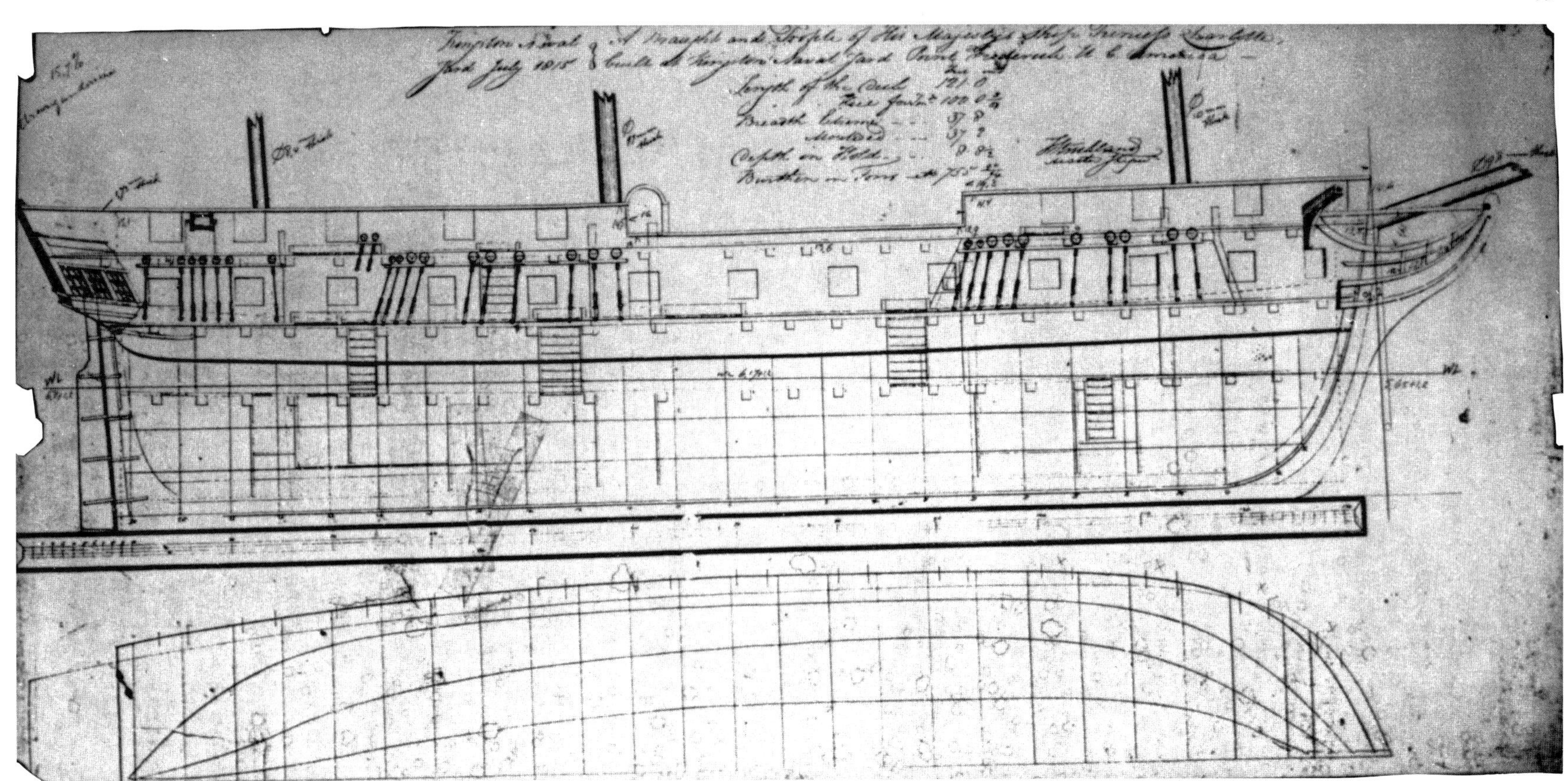

NAC

Pl. 20: Plans of a frigate built in Kingston, similar to the *Sir Isaac Brock*.

fered losses of £388 in stolen or damaged property. Curiously, American soldiers stole "the whole of the Wearing Apparel of Mrs. Givins & 7 Children," and, perhaps more logically, £30 worth of wine and liquor.[68] Other people, such as Penelope Beikie, were not intimidated by looters. Beikie wrote that she "had the temerity to frighten, and even to threaten, some of the enemy" and thereby protect her home from pillage.[69]

The Americans destroyed the printing press of the town's newspaper, *The York Gazette*, and robbed the subscription library and church.[70] (Later in the war, Commodore Chauncey returned some of the books to York.) On April 30, some Americans, probably sailors, set fire to the provincial parliament buildings situated at the east end of York,* along with the neighbouring clerks' offices and the town blockhouse.[71] Others seized General Sheaffe's personal possessions at Government House inside Fort York and subsequently auctioned them to American officers. The official residence itself, already damaged from the explosion of the Grand Magazine, was burned to the ground on May 1, towards the end of the American occupation.[72]

The Americans released the inmates of the town jail, and some of these people assisted in the general pillaging along with other disloyal and lawless elements in the frontier community.[73] American soldiers and sailors threatened and molested some civilians during the occupation. One pillager nearly shot Angelique Givins.[74] A few citizens seemed to have suffered long-term psychological damage from their experience of the occupation. Elizabeth Russell's experience with enemy troops left her so traumatized that more than a year later she showed signs of dejection, like a "mental derangement," whenever rumours circulated of an American return to York.[75] The general lawlessness persuaded the town's magistrates to call a meeting to remind those who had been disloyal that the American occupation was only a temporary affair, that it was "treason to aid, assist, counsel or comfort the Enemy," and that the laws of property ownership remained unchanged, even though the occupying force grossly outnumbered the entire civilian population of York.[76] At the same time, the magistrates swore in some of the town's leading citizens as constables to help protect private property.[77]

The most painful episode of the occupation occurred when the Americans refused to release the British and Canadian wounded from imprisonment in the overcrowded garrison blockhouse where they were kept without food, water, or medical

* The Americans took the speaker's mace and a carved lion that sat in front of the speaker's chair from the parliament buildings as war trophies. They returned the mace to the province in a ceremony at Fort York in 1934 at which memorial plaques also were unveiled to commemorate those who fell in the Battle of York. The mace now is on display at Queen's Park. The lion remains in the United States at the Naval Academy Museum in Annapolis, Maryland.

attention for two days after the battle. In the end, John Strachan convinced Dearborn and Chauncey to release the casualties so he could place them in homes throughout the town for treatment.[78] Meanwhile, the American surgeons did their best to succour their own troops injured in the battle. Dr. Henry Beaumont, a surgeon's mate in the 6th Regiment, along with his fellow surgeons, spent forty-eight hours following the action without food or sleep, "wading in blood, cutting off arms, legs, and trepanning heads to rescue their fellow creatures from untimely deaths."[79]

A large part of the lawlessness committed by the Americans seems to have occurred because General Dearborn and his officers failed to exercise the leadership necessary to keep their men under control. Dearborn himself seems to have been shaken by the battle and behaved irrationally during the occupation. After the surrender, he came ashore, rode up to Colonel Pearce, and asked for a report. When shown the capitulation document, he rode off without saying a word.[80] The next day, he refused to ratify the capitulation – which technically allowed the looting to take place during the first twenty-four hours of the occupation – until John Strachan condemned the American commanders to their faces, saying that the capitulation was a fraud to enable the Americans to claim that they respected private property after they had stolen it. (Interestingly, Colonel Chewett and Major Allan had disappeared from the scene during this tense period, and Strachan alone represented the town's interests to the Americans.) The day after the battle, a rumour spread through York that Sheaffe was about to counter-attack. Dearborn had the drums beat the call to arms, but, instead of mounting a horse to take command of his brigade, he merely walked behind the troops with his hands behind his back in what seems to have been a confused or depressed state. In the end, Colonel Pearce persuaded him that the rumour was false and Dearborn had the men return to Fort York. (It was Pearce, not Dearborn, who initially agreed to Strachan's request to distribute food to the militia prisoners on April 28.) Later during the occupation, when Strachan protested that the looting continued after the Americans ratified the capitulation, Dearborn took no action, but merely complained that the pillaging was contrary to his strictest orders. When Strachan asked Dearborn for protection for Angelique Givins, whose life had been threatened, Dearborn only recommended that she not return home because it was out of his power to protect anyone associated with Aboriginal peoples. (Her husband was the Indian Department agent who served with the Mississaugas and Ojibways during the battle.)[81]

During the occupation, a Sergeant Derby and four other men of the 8th Regiment of Foot, who had fought in the battle, returned to York surreptitiously in a bateau to recover weapons and knapsacks that had been left behind. The British soldiers succeeded but did not get very far when their bateau began to leak. Derby beached the vessel and returned to York a second

MTL, T13800

Pl. 21: The war caused severe strain for the people of York. Ann Strachan (1784-1865) and her young children fled to Cornwall in eastern Upper Canada where they thought they would be safer than in the capital. However, American troops marched through that town, robbed Ann (who was pregnant), and molested her in such a way as to leave her emotionally and physically sick for months afterwards. This silhouette dates to 1807.

time to get a barge that had belonged to Isaac Brock. After taking it from under the noses of American guards stationed at the lighthouse on the Peninsula, he picked up the equipment from the bateau and sailed to Kingston.[82]

Towards the evening of May 2, most of the Americans, except for some stragglers who were picked up by their officers later, boarded their ships and schooners in preparation to leave York .[83] Bad weather kept the Americans at anchor in the harbour until May 8 when they sailed off towards Niagara to attack Fort George.[84] However, that attack had to be postponed for two weeks because an outbreak of diarrhoea and dysentery among the troops forced Dearborn to sail back to Sackett's Harbor.[85] The Americans may have been fortunate in leaving York when they did. At the time of the attack, a messenger went to the Iroquois communities along the Grand River, 100 kilometres west of York, to ask for their help. Between 300 and 400 Iroquois chiefs and warriors then marched towards York, prepared to launch surprise attacks or other actions as the situation allowed, but the Americans had left York by the time the Iroquois got to Burlington, fifty kilometres away, and the Iroquois cancelled the expedition.[86]

After the Americans departed, the townspeople walked to the garrison to survey the battlefield. They found the British dead buried "a few inches below the earth," but the indefatigable John Strachan "gave them christian burial" while "all assisted to secure their graves from further disturbance."[87]

THE IMPACT OF THE BATTLE OF YORK

The New York Republicans did not benefit directly from the attack on York as it occurred on the first of the three-day polling period for the New York State election. However, the victory proclamations circulated prior to the attack, the support of soldier voters, and military spending in the state seemed to have contributed to the re-election of the pro-war Republican governor, Daniel Tompkins, by a narrow 3,606-vote margin – his smallest margin in three gubernatorial races. In most parts of the state, the opposing candidates received about the same number of votes, except in the western districts where the army's presence and government spending seemed to have been the decisive factor in giving the Republicans the lead. The Federalists won a slight majority in the House of Assembly.[88]

Militarily, the Americans were disappointed in not capturing either the *Sir Isaac Brock* or the *Prince Regent*. Yet, the destruction of the *Brock* was a partial triumph since Dearborn did not necessarily expect to capture the frigate and had told the American secretary of war that he wanted to "take or destroy the armed vessels at York."[89] The loss of the *Brock* hurt British naval efforts on Lake Ontario by preventing the Royal Navy from gaining ascendancy on the lake until late in 1814.[90] As a result, the British squadron neither transported all the supplies needed for the troops and Native allies on the Niagara Peninsula, nor prevented Chauncey's squadron from supporting the American army in the Niagara region. Ultimately, the Americans did not exploit their advantage fully and the British army prevented the Americans from conquering Canadian territory along the Niagara River by the end of the war.

The Americans did capture an old schooner in York, the *Duke of Gloucester*, but it was not much more than a hulk that had been used as a floating prison in Toronto Bay. Dearborn dismissed it as unfit for use although he towed it back to Sackett's Harbor.[91] There was a privately owned schooner in York that was exempt from capture by the terms of capitulation, but the Americans did not want the British to use it, so they burned it and compensated its owner with £300 from the provincial treasury, which they had seized during the occupation.[92] (Sheaffe had the treasury hidden the night before the attack, but the Americans threatened to destroy York unless the townspeople turned it over. The money, £2,145, was in army bills* rather than coin and probably was of limited use to the Americans.)[93]

Large quantities of naval supplies destined for the British Lake Erie squadron either were destroyed by the retreating British or were captured by the Americans. The loss of the supplies was a significant contributing factor in the defeat of that squad-

* Army bills were paper notes issued during the war to facilitate the purchase of goods and services and were redeemable in coin or specie from the government.

ron by the larger American force in a very close battle in September 1813.[94] The Americans followed up that victory by defeating a British and Native force on the Thames River in southwestern Upper Canada. The net effect of those battles was the loss of much of the Lake Erie region until 1815 when the Americans returned the territory in compliance with the Treaty of Ghent, which ended the war. The Americans did not use the captured naval supplies themselves: they ditched some in Toronto Bay before leaving York, and those they took back to Sackett's Harbor were set on fire during the British attack on the American naval base in May 1813.[95]

Lieutenant-Colonel William Chewett and his officers in the York Militia – who contributed to the British defeat at York by not bringing their men into action when ordered – spent the weeks following the battle shifting the blame to General Sheaffe to cover up their own disobedience and culpability.[96] Through their bitter accusations of incompetence and their political connections, they were able to have Sheaffe removed from civil and military command in Upper Canada.

Many Canadians demanded revenge for the destruction of civil and private property in York.[97] After the burning of York's public buildings, the American army committed other vicious acts against the civilian population of Upper Canada, such as burning the town of Niagara on a cold winter's night in December 1813, an act that led Upper Canadians as a whole to demand revenge. Sir George Prevost responded to the outcry by asking Vice-Admiral Sir Alexander Cochrane on the Atlantic front to punish the Americans. In one letter, he wrote: "You may ... assist in inflicting that measure of retaliation which shall deter the enemy from a repetition of similar outrages."[98] Cochrane took up Prevost's request and issued orders to his subordinates to retaliate: "You are hereby required and directed to destroy and lay waste such towns and districts as you may find assailable. You will hold strictly in view the conduct of the American army towards His Majesty's unoffending Canadian subjects, and you will spare merely the lives of the unarmed American inhabitants of the United States. For only by carrying this retaliation into the country of our enemy can we hope to make him sensible of the impolicy as well as the inhumanity of the system he has adopted."[99]

Canadians got their revenge in August 1814. The British army landed near Washington, defeated the American army in the Battle of Blandensburg, then marched into Washington. During their brief two-day occupation, they burned the White House, Congress, and other government buildings in retaliation for the destruction of the governor's residence and parliament buildings in York. When rebuilt in 1817, the burn marks on the White House were whitewashed. This gave rise to a popular story that the president's mansion received its name from the repainting. In fact, the name "White House" pre-dates the war and originated

ROYAL ONTARIO MUSEUM, 990.49.8

Pl. 22: Robert Irvine's watercolour shows the condition of some of the British and American vessels after the Battle of Lake Erie. Painted a few days after the action, Irvine shows, from left to right: HMS *Queen Charlotte*, USS *Niagara*, HMS *Detroit*, and USS *Lawrence*.

because the whitish limestone construction of the mansion contrasted with the red brick used in neighbouring buildings.

After the British army destroyed the American government buildings, opposition members of the British parliament denounced the burning as being beneath the dignity of a civilized nation such as Great Britain. In the government's defence, Prime Minister Lord Liverpool and Chancellor of the Exchequer Nicholas Vansittart replied that the action was a retaliatory act for the destruction of the parliament buildings and government house in York.[100] Back in British North America, Sir George Prevost told Canadians that "as a just retribution, the proud capital at Washington has experienced a similar fate to that inflicted by an American force on the seat of government in Upper Canada."[101] In York, John Strachan summarized Canadian feelings when he wrote that the destruction of Washington "was a small retaliation after redress had been refused for burnings and depredations, not only of public but private property" in Canada.[102]

THE SECOND ATTACK ON YORK

The Americans did not try to hold York after capturing the town in April because it had little military value to them and because occupying the post was beyond their logistical capabilities at that moment. Although they burned the parliament buildings, Government House, its outbuildings, the naval yard, and the garrison and town blockhouses, they left the barracks standing.[103] Presumably they thought that they would need them later in the year for an occupying army after conquering Upper Canada. Shortly after the April capture of York, British forces repossessed the town, but these troops would have been at a serious disadvantage during another attack without the blockhouses and other defences.

The second phase of Dearborn's strategy, the invasion of the Niagara Peninsula, collapsed by July. In May, the Americans sailed from Sackett's Harbor again and captured Fort George at the mouth of the Niagara River as the first step in taking the Niagara region. But in June, when they tried to follow up this success by expelling the British and their Native allies from the peninsula, they suffered defeat at two battles, Stoney Creek and Beaver Dams. The British next advanced on Fort George. By July, the Americans found themselves blockaded in Fort George by a smaller but more aggressive British, Canadian, and Native force under Sheaffe's successor, Major-General Baron Francis de Rottenburg.

To relieve the pressure on Fort George, the Americans decided to strike the main British supply depot on the Niagara Peninsula on Burlington Heights (at today's Dundurn Castle in Hamilton). Thirteen vessels of the American squadron, augmented with 500 soldiers under the command of Lieutenant-

NYHS

Pl. 23: Before entering Washington in 1814, the British army defeated the Americans at Blandensburg. This fanciful contemporary print gives the wrong impression of the scale of the battle, derisively called the "Blandensburg Races" in reference to how fast the American army ran away from the British forces.

Colonel Winfield Scott, were assigned to make the raid. The British suspected American intentions when they spotted the squadron cruising off Burlington in late July. To reinforce the depot, the bulk of the troops then in York rushed to the beach behind Burlington Heights. This force, under Lieutenant-Colonel Francis Battersby, consisted of a "demi-brigade" of light infantry comprising components of the Glengarry Light Infantry, four companies of the Canadian Voltigeurs, and the light companies of the 1st, 8th, 49th, and 104th Regiments of Foot, as well as some artillery.[104] Since this move made York vulnerable, Battersby took with him to Burlington cattle in York intended to feed the army.[105]

The Americans landed at Burlington Beach (in modern-day Burlington) on July 29 but re-embarked without attempting a battle when they saw the size of the force sent to meet them.[106] Thus, the reinforcements from York helped preserve the critically important supply depot and enabled Baron de Rottenburg to keep the Americans cornered in Fort George.

Battersby's move left York unprotected. The American squadron sailed to York, arriving in the harbour on July 31. The militia could not fight because they still were on parole from the Battle of York. Many of the townspeople fled to the neighbouring forests for fear that the Americans would round up the militiamen and take them to prisoner of war camps in the United States.[107] The total number of troops in York consisted of only one small troop of the 19th Light Dragoons.[108] Resistance was impossible, so the cavalrymen gathered together all the military supplies they could and withdrew up the Don River.[109]

The Americans landed 340 men and burned the barracks at the fort, the blockhouses on Gibraltar Point, and the military fuel yard to deprive the British of good accommodation at York.[110] They also let the inmates out of the jail, made prisoners of the soldiers in the jail and the hospital, paroled the wounded who could not be moved, took what government stores they could find, and looted some private property (again assisted by disloyal citizens). That night, they re-embarked on their ships and schooners.[111]

A traitorous citizen in York told the Americans about the supplies hidden by the dragoons. (In September 1813, information was laid against thirty-two residents of York and the neighbouring settlements for seditious activities during the two occupations. Disloyalty on the part of American immigrants living north of York was an ongoing problem, and the local militia regularly patrolled the region throughout the war to assert government authority.)[112] Informed about the dragoons, the Americans sent three armed boats up the Don River to take what they could. However, the cavalrymen spirited most of the supplies away, losing very little to the enemy. The Americans set sail later that day, leaving York on August 1.[113]

FORT YORK REBUILT

On the morning of August 26, 1813, Lieutenant-Colonel Ralph Bruyères arrived in York to begin the process of rebuilding the town's fortifications.[114] He wanted to start with the construction of blockhouses, to be built away from the waterfront because there was a shortage of cannon, which made a lakeside defence against a naval bombardment difficult. Remembering the first attack on York in which the United States Navy played a key role in protecting the American army through a barrage on the British positions, Bruyères believed a site a few hundred metres inland would be better because it would force American troops to land and operate without naval support, thus making an enemy attack more likely to fail. However, Bruyères could not persuade his superiors to accept this plan, and reconstruction of the town's defences began on the present site of Fort York – the original 1793 location – when a detachment of the Royal Sappers and Miners arrived in York shortly afterwards.[115]

Towards the end of November 1813, the Royal Engineers reported that there were two functional batteries in place at Fort York. They rebuilt the Government House Battery as the present Circular Battery and mounted two 8-inch (20.3 cm) mortars in it.* They also rebuilt the battery in the Garrison Creek ravine just east of today's fort by the water's edge. Because of the shortage of artillery, the army re-incorporated one of Simcoe's guns – not considered good enough by the Americans to take away in April or July – into this battery beside a new 12-pounder. Construction was almost finished on the oldest surviving buildings in today's fort, Blockhouses Numbers 1 and 2.[116] Unmentioned in the engineer's report, but showing clearly on a map drawn at that time, was the current west wall of the fort, constructed in 1811.[117] In addition, the Royal Engineers seem to have intended to build a masonry tower at Fort York to strengthen the harbour defences, but they did not carry the project through, although stone had been delivered to the site.[118] (Plans for it do not survive. It may have been a two- or three-storey bomb-proof building with a gun deck on its roof similar to the one that survives today at Fort Mississauga in Niagara-on-the-Lake.)

At or near the site of the old Western Battery, a new Western Battery, protected by earthworks, a three-metre-high loopholed palisade, and a defensible guardhouse, helped guard the harbour entrance. It mounted two 24-pounder guns and two 24-pounder carronades.[119] Behind Fort York (at today's Trinity-Bellwoods Park), a new blockhouse guarded the main road into town from the west as well as the fort's rear. This blockhouse mounted a long 12-pounder and one of Simcoe's condemned 9-pounders on an

* Mortars fired exploding shells at a high trajectory, in contrast to guns, which normally fired solid iron shot on a relatively straight trajectory.

open gun deck on its roof. The engineers used much heavier timbers in its construction than in the fort blockhouses to support the weight and recoil shock of the guns.[120] On Gibraltar Point, a new blockhouse covered the south side of the harbour entrance and protected the Peninsula. Earthworks surrounded the road and Peninsula blockhouses, making them small forts in their own right.[121] Earthworks at the Don River guarded the Kingston Road into York from the east from attack. Although relatively light compared to the defences at the western approaches to York, these earthworks probably were adequate because the American navy could not support the army in an attack from that direction because the Peninsula served as an effective barrier to shipping at the east end of York.

Construction at Fort York occurred more slowly than the army would have liked because of a severe shortage of artificers (military craftsmen) and labourers to work on the fortifications. Bruyères complained that he had only thirteen carpenters working for him in 1814 instead of the fifty he needed. The winter of 1813-1814 also presented problems because there was very little snow on the ground, a condition that hindered the transportation of supplies since sleighs could not be used to carry materials to York.[122] Construction continued through 1814, 1815, and possibly 1816 to enclose the fort with a defensive wall, to erect batteries and buildings in the fort and at other strategic locations, to improve the military roads in and out of York, and to clear the forest near the fortifications to deprive the Americans of cover in the event of another attack.[123] Today's North and South Barracks, Officers' Barracks and Mess, and magazines date from these years.

THE THIRD AMERICAN DESCENT ON YORK

The rebuilding of the harbour defences was important because a four-vessel squadron operated out of Toronto Bay in support of the British forces on the Niagara Peninsula in 1814. Commanded by Captain Alexander Dobbs of the Royal Navy, the squadron moved supplies and troops to the Niagara front and brought wounded and exhausted soldiers back to York. Without defences, the vessels at York would have been vulnerable to capture. The loss of the squadron would have been disastrous as it would have forced the British to rely on the 125 kilometres of miserable roads between York and Niagara to supply the troops at the front instead of the fast fifty-kilometre water route across the lake.[124]

On August 6, 1814, lookouts on the American Lake Ontario squadron sighted the British fourteen-gun schooner, HMS *Magnet*, as she sailed towards Niagara. Driven ashore ten kilometres from Fort George, her captain set her on fire and blew her up to prevent the Americans from capturing the vessel.[125] The American naval commander suspected that the *Magnet* had come

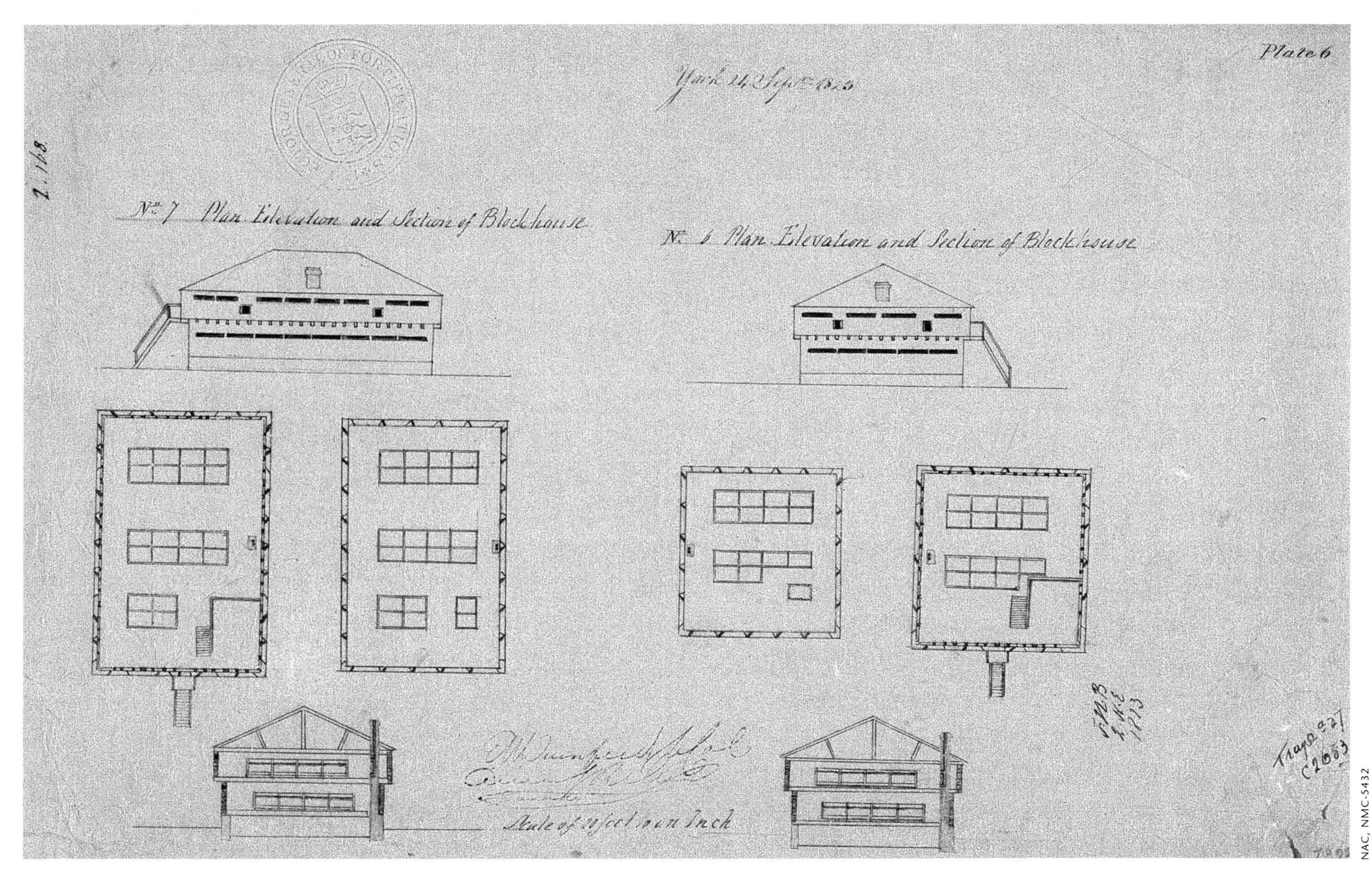

NAC, NMC-5432

Pl. 24: The first buildings constructed at Fort York following the second attack were Blockhouses Numbers 1 and 2. Begun in September 1813, they seem to have been finished before the new year. This plan dates to 1823.

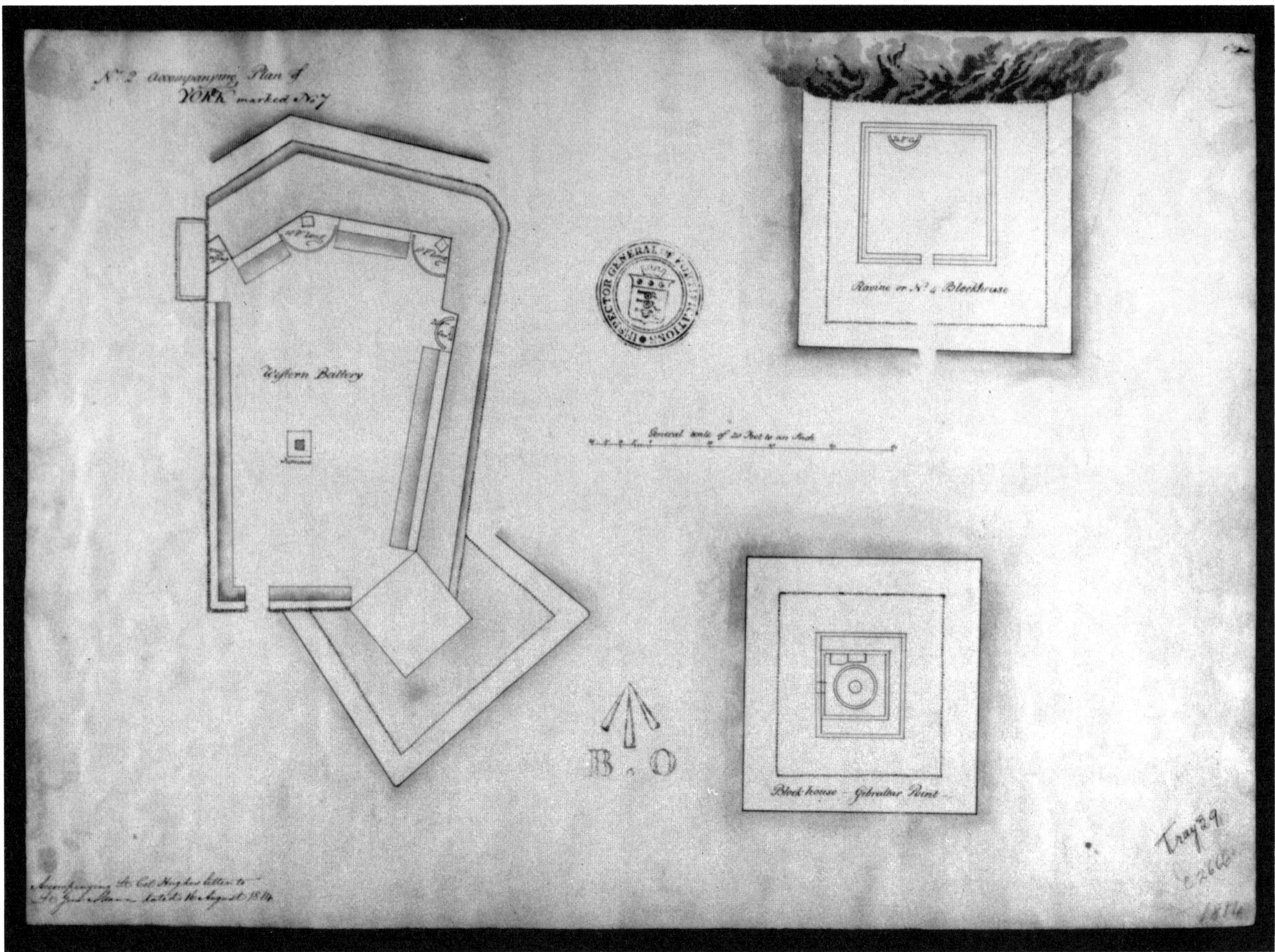

NAC, NMC-5431

Map 6: Plans of the Western Battery, Ravine Blockhouse, and Gibraltar Point Blockhouse in 1814. The furnace in the Western Battery could heat cannon balls to red-hot temperatures to set enemy ships on fire. Note the open gun decks on the roofs of the blockhouses.

from York and wanted to determine if there were other ships or schooners to be captured at the provincial capital. He decided to send one of his vessels, the *Lady of the Lake*, into the harbour under a flag of truce on some pretext to spy out the situation before attacking. The militiamen stationed at Fort York – released from the parole they had signed after the first attack – were not about to let that happen. They scrambled to the guns and opened fire. The American schooner hoisted her colours and returned fire before withdrawing out of range to join her sister vessels.[126]

For the next three days, as the Americans hovered outside the harbour, citizens packed up their loved ones and possessions, as they had done in 1813, and fled the town. Soldiers convalescing in the hospitals took up their weapons, and reinforcements from the 6th and 82nd Regiments of Foot hurried to York and Burlington to bolster the militia.[127] In the end, the Americans decided not to challenge Fort York's new defences but sailed away instead. The rebuilt Fort York and its outlying defences had fulfilled the classic military function of deterrence.

THE END OF THE WAR

Although the Americans won a number of battles in 1813, their efforts to conquer Upper Canada in the second year of the war ended in failure, except for the occupation of part of southwestern Upper Canada following the battles of Lake Erie and the Thames. After the collapse of the Niagara Peninsula campaign, American commanders withdrew most of their troops eastward for a two-pronged attack on Montréal in the autumn. The British defeated these forces in the battles of Crysler's Farm and Châteauguay. Towards the end of the year, the remaining Americans on the Niagara front retreated out of Fort George and returned to Fort Niagara on the American side of the border. The British quickly re-occupied Fort George, then launched a surprise night attack on Fort Niagara in December, captured it, and drove American forces out of the Niagara Peninsula before the end of the year.

In 1814, the American army again invaded Upper Canada, crossing the Niagara River at Buffalo, capturing Fort Erie early in July, and defeating the British at the Battle of Chippawa two days later. However, the British won the Battle of Lundy's Lane that followed, forced the Americans back to Fort Erie, and then placed the American garrison under siege. After successfully holding the fort for a number of months, the Americans blew it up and withdrew to Buffalo. With this withdrawal, the 1814 American invasion of Upper Canada came to a failed end. In the far west, the Americans failed to recapture Mackinac from the British; the British, using that post as a base, maintained control over most of the far west (Wisconsin, Illinois, Indiana, and part of Michigan).

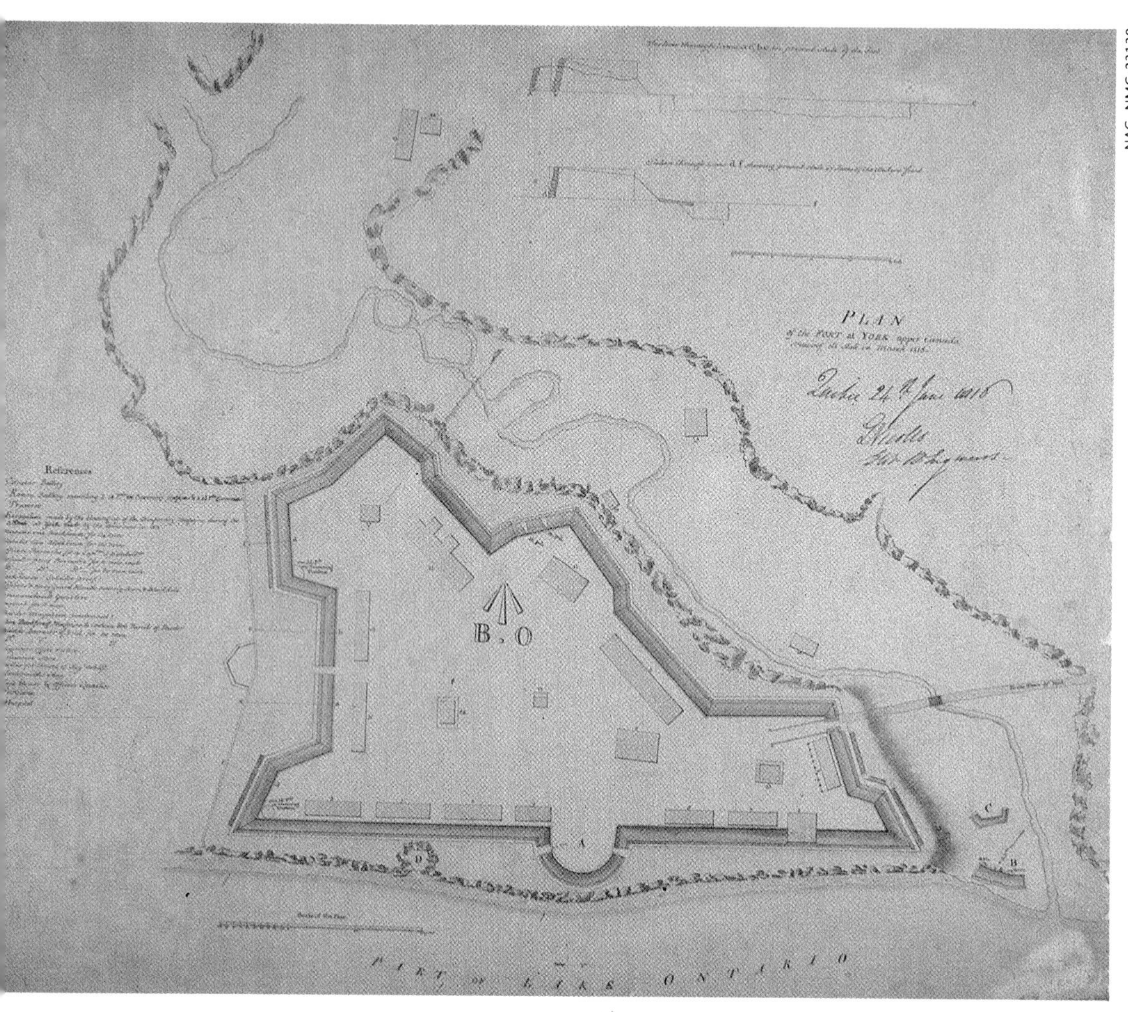

NAC, NMC-23139

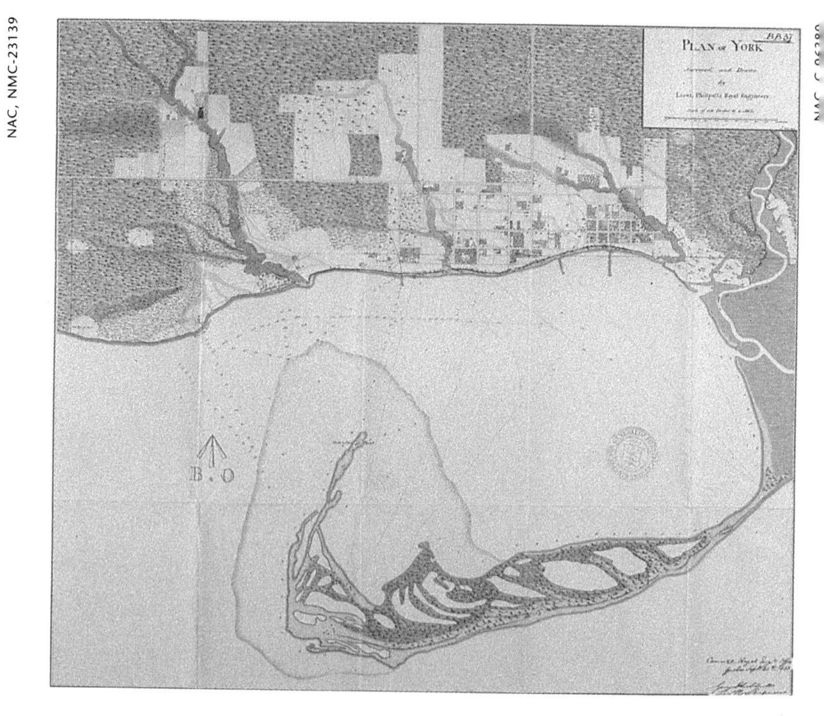

(Above) **Map 8: As this 1818 map shows, the water near Gibraltar Point was too shallow for ships and schooners, so enemy vessels had to pass close under the guns of Fort York to enter the harbour.**

(Left) **Map 7: This 1816 plan shows Fort York just after the war, on the original 1793 site, and illustrates the use of the local geography to improve the fort's defensive posture. Also visible on the Lake Ontario side of the fort is the crater left from the explosion of the Grand Magazine during the Battle of York.**

York served as a hospital centre for the Niagara Peninsula forces from the time of the Battle of Stoney Creek in June 1813.[128] Casualties were transported to York for treatment beyond what was available in the field. It usually took two or three days to move a wounded soldier from the Niagara area to York. Medical facilities were crowded in the capital, and other buildings, such as the town's church, had to be turned into temporary hospitals by the summer of 1813.[129] John Strachan, who visited the hospitals regularly, noted that many soldiers were "sadly mangled" and died while undergoing treatment.[130] During periods of heavy fighting on the Niagara Peninsula, Strachan found himself burying as many as six or eight men each day in the garrison graveyard (now Victoria Memorial Square to the northeast of Fort York).[131]

By 1813, with the development of a more favourable military situation in the European war against Napoléon, the British redeployed some of their military forces to take offensive action against the United States. First, they imposed a crippling naval blockade of the American coast. By 1814, this blockade was so effective that American international trade dropped by 90% from its pre-war levels.[132] Second, in 1814, the British sent significant numbers of soldiers to North America after defeating the French in Europe. As a result, British troops not only secured Canada, but attacked the United States in an effort to bring the war to an end by putting pressure directly on American territory. Although

MTL, T13801

Pl. 25: John Strachan (1778-1867) worked tirelessly in the military hospitals during the summer of 1814 when casualties were particularly numerous. The gruesome state of the wounded and the fact that he buried six or eight men each day led him to lament, "I wish that those who are so ready stirring up wars would traverse the field of battle after an engagement or visit the hospitals next day and they would receive a lesson that might be very beneficial to them in future." The silhouette dates to 1807.

these raids were of limited success (Washington and part of Maine were captured, but the Americans defended Plattsburg, Baltimore, and New Orleans successfully), the attacks helped increase opposition to the war in the United States and speed peace negotiations then underway in Belgium.

The War of 1812 came to an end with the ratification of the Treaty of Ghent of December 1814. News of the treaty reached York in February 1815. It was good news. The war had ended, and the American invasion of Canada had been repulsed. The expulsion of the Americans from Canada (including southwestern Upper Canada, which the American army evacuated as part of the treaty conditions), combined with the superior performance of the British forces during the war, told Upper Canadians that Great Britain had won the War of 1812.*

Nevertheless, construction at Fort York continued because of continued fears the Americans would try to conquer Upper Canada since they had failed to do so during the war. By the end of 1815 or early in 1816, the fort was completed adequately for peacetime requirements. The main garrison consisted of eighteen buildings: seven soldiers' barracks, three officers' quarters, two blockhouses, two magazines, one guardhouse, a cookhouse, and one engineer's office and store. These buildings, designed to hold 650 officers and men, were surrounded by heavy earthen walls, capable of absorbing incoming cannon shot, and were partially supplemented by fraises, or horizontal palisades, located half-way up these walls to keep out a land assault. In wartime, more guns could be added at strategic points to the nine already in place in the fort. Fraises could be expanded and upright palisades could be added to the bottom of the walls.[133] As already noted, additional defensive features protected the harbour entrance and other strategic locations. A hospital, blacksmith's shop, storehouses, and other military facilities stood just to the north of the fort in the creek valley and east along Front Street on the waterfront. The buildings outside the fort could house an extra 350 officers and men.

Despite the willingness of military authorities to rebuild and maintain a garrison at York after the return of peace, the war dealt the death blow to all aspirations to turn the provincial capital into a major naval base. Most important in thwarting the plan was the capture of the town in April and July 1813 in contrast to

* Across the border, Americans also were immensely relieved that the war had ended. Through a curious leap in logic, however, they forgot their reasons for going to war and the failure of their army to conquer Canada. Instead, they chose to focus on the successful defence of Baltimore, Plattsburg, and New Orleans, thus deceiving themselves into thinking they somehow had won a "second war of independence" against British efforts to reverse the outcome of the American Revolution! To bolster their arguments, they pointed to the resolution of the maritime disputes between Britain and the United States as proof of their success. Conveniently overlooked was the fact that it was Britain's victory over France, not American actions, that ended the Royal Navy's needs to impress seamen and blockade Europe.

ST. LAWRENCE PARKS COMMISSION

Pl. 26: The rebuilding of Kingston's Fort Henry in the 1830s demonstrated clearly that military planners considered Kingston to be far more important than York in the defence of Upper Canada.

the Americans' unwillingness even to attempt a serious assault against Kingston. As well, wartime exigencies led to an expansion of Kingston's naval facilities and defences, which helped to solidify that town's role as Upper Canada's main naval base. Furthermore, there were some strategists who thought York's new defences were too limited to offer much protection. One authority, who obviously had a philosophical disagreement with Colonel Bruyères's design of York's new fortifications, believed that sharpshooters could get behind Fort York and silence the fort's guns "in half an hour."[134] Given the nature of the local geography, this does not seem to have been likely, but these disparaging arguments undoubtedly had their effect, especially since they came from the provisional lieutenant-governor of the province, Sir Frederick Philipse Robinson. Exaggerated comments aside, York's fortifications were not strong enough to serve as a major provincial bastion although they more or less were capable of meeting local needs, as had been demonstrated in August 1814.

CHAPTER THREE

FORT YORK AND THE TORONTO GARRISON, 1815–1945

THE POST-WAR GARRISON

Following the War of 1812, military planners on both sides of the border agreed on the reason the United States failed to conquer Upper Canada: the Americans did not sever the St. Lawrence River supply line by capturing either Kingston or Montréal. One droll British strategist wrote, "In the conduct of the three campaigns, a most wonderful deficiency of military knowledge and judgment, had been displayed on the part of the American generals."[1]

In anticipation of future hostilities, the British concentrated defence construction in that exposed region. They upgraded fortifications south of Montréal to stop an attack along the Lake Champlain-Richelieu River route. In Kingston, the army replaced Fort Henry with a massive citadel in the 1830s and further improved Kingston's defences in the 1840s by constructing a number of Martello Towers and other works during the Oregon Boundary Dispute.* (Martello Towers were circular stone coastal fortifications mounting heavy artillery.) Most ambitious of all, the British government built the Rideau Canal to create an alternative water route to the vulnerable St. Lawrence River. With these works, the British hoped supply lines could be kept open and reinforcements could be dispatched to Upper Canada

* Britain and the United States jointly occupied the Oregon territory. However, in 1845, American Democrats suggested that the United States should assume exclusive control of the region. In the end, the two powers agreed to divide the territory along the 49th parallel instead of the more northerly 54th parallel, which the Americans wanted.

MTL, T13445

Pl. 27: Murney Tower, a Martello Tower in Kingston photographed in the late nineteenth century, was built in the 1840s. During an attack, the roof would be removed to allow the guns on the upper level, mounted on tracks for easy manoeuvre, to fire. Note the drawbridge on the right side of the photograph spanning a deep ditch surrounding the tower. Towers similar to this were recommended for the defence of Toronto harbour throughout much of the nineteenth century.

quickly to retake any territory lost in central or western Upper Canada in the early stages of a war. Military strategists in the post-war era saw two roles for York. First, it was a position that either could cover a retreating army from the Niagara Peninsula, or could serve as a rallying point for the defence of the Niagara region. Second, it could protect communications along the Toronto Passage with the military and naval posts on the upper Great Lakes, such as Penetanguishene and Drummond Island.[2]

During the post-war years, the army demolished some of the buildings at Fort York and built new ones. The fortifications were not maintained well during periods of relative peace and therefore eroded or otherwise deteriorated. But, at the first sign of possible hostilities, the army rebuilt and strengthened Fort York's walls and batteries. The number of troops at Fort York changed with the state of international relations, too. About 200 or 300 men typically garrisoned Fort York during the peaceful 1820s, whereas the army posted over 600 regulars (as well as militia) in Toronto in 1838 during the tense period of the Rebellion Crisis. At the time of the Crimean War in 1854, the army virtually abandoned Toronto for a short period when Britain tried to scrape together a respectable army from her scattered Empire to fight the Russians.[3] Some American threats were less serious than others. Often anti-British bellicosity on the part of American politicians was only a ploy to win the votes of Anglophobic Irish immigrants during elections.[4]

NAC, C-99558

Pl. 28: This 1821 view of Fort York from the east shows the dramatic prominence of the fort in relation to the surrounding environment. Note the strength of the walls and the closeness of the lake. ("The Fort at York" by John Elliott Woolford.)

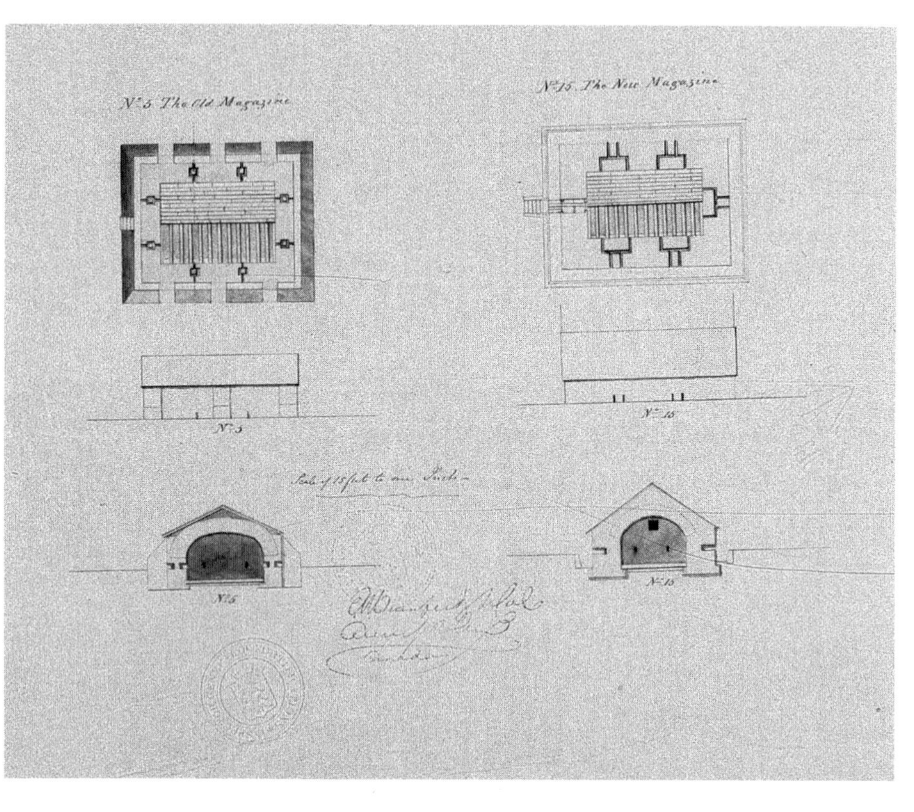

NAC, NMC-5361

Pl. 29: These 1823 plans are the earliest surviving images of the gunpowder magazines at Fort York. The one of the left, the East Magazine, dates from 1814. Its original heavy bomb-proof roof caused the supporting walls to buckle and it had to be condemned. In 1824, the army removed the roof and converted the magazine into a storage building. The plan on the right is the 1815 Stone Magazine.

Factors other than American threats also determined the size of the Toronto garrison. Among them was opposition in Britain to maintaining large garrisons abroad when local colonial governments would not assume a significant share of their own defence costs, or when enemies elsewhere in the world posed more serious threats than the Americans did, or when European tensions raised the possibility of an invasion of the United Kingdom itself.* The vast improvement in transportation that occurred in the nineteenth century was another factor affecting the size of the local garrison. In 1846, Britain's colonial secretary, Earl Grey, suggested that the fast new ocean-going steamships eliminated the need to post large numbers of troops abroad because soldiers could be dispatched quickly to any troubled spot, in contrast to earlier days when sailing ships might take many weeks to make an ocean crossing.[5] Within colonies, the development of canals and railways in the middle decades of the nineteenth century reduced from weeks to mere days the time it took for troops to move hundreds of kilometres. However, some people argued

* For example, between 1848 and 1852, people in Britain became alarmed when they learned that the army within the United Kingdom was too small to defend Britain from French invasion. In 1858, a light year for military spending, Britain spent £261,000 for Canadian defence while the Province of Canada allocated only £40,000. In contrast, the British spent £44,000 on the defence of Victoria in Australia while that colony's government allocated £94,000 even though it had no potential enemy on its borders.

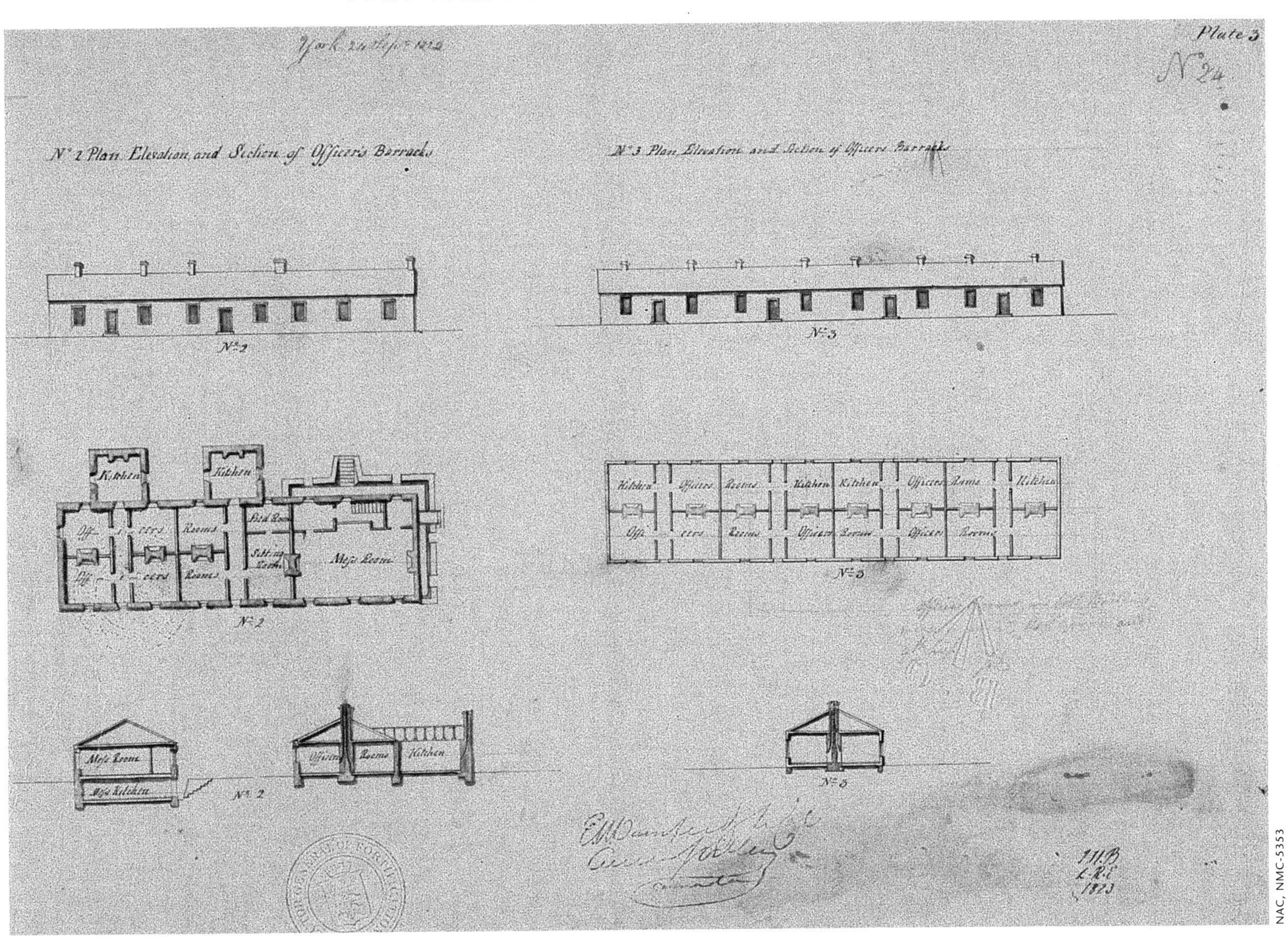

NAC, NMC-5353

Pl. 30: An 1823 plan of the Officers' Brick Barracks and Mess Establishment (left) and the Junior Officers' Barracks or Blue Barracks (right). The 1815 Brick Barracks survives to this day while the Blue Barracks is represented at Fort York by a 1930s reproduction (but which contains a significant quantity of original materials in its construction).

COURTESY OF THE DIRECTOR, NATIONAL ARMY MUSEUM, LONDON

Pl. 31: Soldiers of the 71st Highland Light Infantry dressed for the Canadian winter in the late 1840s. The 71st garrisoned Fort York between 1829 and 1831 and again between 1850 and 1852. Stationed in Kingston after Toronto, they were one of the regiments dispatched from North America to the Crimea at the outbreak of war with Russia in 1854.

against placing too much confidence in new transportation systems instead of strong garrisons because the crucial east-west canals and railways could be destroyed if the Americans gained control of part of the St. Lawrence River for even a brief period during a conflict.[6]

The British army maintained a presence in Toronto more or less continuously for fifty-six years following the War of 1812 as part of its responsibility to defend Canada from any renewed American attempts to annex the colonies and to assist civil authorities in maintaining law and order. The regiments stationed at Fort York in the post-war years included several famous regiments, such as the 71st Highland Light Infantry, the Royal Canadian Rifle Regiment, and the 13th Hussars. The civilian community itself grew substantially after the war. In 1815, York had a population of 700. By 1834, when the Town of York incorporated as the City of Toronto, the population was 9,000. It reached 30,000 by 1851 and continued to grow, reaching 56,000 by the time the last British troops left the city in 1870. As the city expanded and its economy became more diversified, the military's impact on Toronto diminished, but always remained significant while Fort York housed an imperial garrison.

Not only did the soldiers call the garrison home, so did their wives and children who shared barrack space with their husbands and fathers. In 1829, for example, the garrison consisted of 276 officers and men from the 68th Regiment of Foot and eight sol-

MTL, T13753

Pl. 32: Officers of the 30th Regiment of Foot in front of the 1829 Parliament Buildings on Front Street. The 30th garrisoned Toronto from 1861 to 1863.

diers of the Royal Artillery. There were fifteen women and sixty children associated with the 68th – a figure that probably did not include officers' families – and the Royal Artillery had one woman and two children living in Fort York.[7] There even was a "lying-in room" in one of the barracks for women to use at the birth of their children.[8]

A school served the children of the garrison as well as soldiers who wanted to learn to read and write. A garrison library opened in 1841 (replacing earlier unofficial and hospital libraries) in an effort to improve the quality of life for the common soldier. The first librarian was a Sergeant Trout of the 43rd Light Infantry, and 144 books formed part of the library's first shipment from England. By 1845, the number of books had grown to 566.[9] Novels seemed to have been the soldiers' favourites. In 1859, the inspector-general of army schools sniffed that common soldiers, being "incapable of appreciating books written for educated readers," preferred authors such as Jane Austen, James Fenimore Cooper, Henry Fielding, and Sir Walter Scott![10] Libraries and schools, along with sports fields and other amenities, were part of a general trend to improve the lot of the common soldier and his family as the nineteenth century wore on. In 1815, for example, each of the six rooms of the two brick soldiers' barracks housed as many as thirty-two adults and their children. Between 1829 and 1834, one room became a sergeants' mess, each of the other five had their populations reduced to eighteen adults and their children, and military authorities made requests to increase the fuel allowance to make the rooms warmer.[11] In the 1860s, the army segregated soldiers with families from unmarried men at Fort York, with two or three families being assigned to one barrack room. A few years later, after the creation of a Canadian army, each of the barrack rooms was subdivided into small rooms for the exclusive use of one family, and kitchens were built on the back of these apartments.[12] Though these circumstances were poor compared to modern standards, the common soldiers generally came from the lowest ranks of British and Canadian society where conditions were so impoverished that army accommodation usually was superior to what recruits had experienced in civilian life. Despite these efforts, most officers considered the fort's barracks to be sub-standard, and over the years they made requests for new facilities for the troops in York.

In contrast to the rank and file, the officers generally – but not exclusively – came from the middle and upper levels of British and colonial society. They lived in relative comfort compared to the other ranks, although they too complained about the poor quality of their barracks on a regular basis.[13] In 1837, for example, a group of officers inspected the rooms in the Officers' Brick Barracks and noted that the rooms were small, gloomy, damp, and ill-ventilated.[14] Married officers regularly took quarters in the town rather than in the fort as did some single officers who could afford to live away from the garrison.

MTL, T30655

Pl. 33: St. John the Evangelist Anglican Church – the "Garrison Church" as it appeared in 1859, a year after construction. This building sat just north of the original 1793-1860 military cemetery to the northeast of Fort York. The wood building was replaced by a brick church in 1893 (no longer extant). The cemetery is now Victoria Memorial Square, about two blocks northeast of Fort York.

MTL, T13382

The officers of the garrison were famous for hosting dances, sleighing parties, and theatricals. One such entertainment was a ball and supper at Fort York in 1828, hosted by the officers of the 68th Foot. A newspaper account of the party noted, "The Mess-Room and the quarters of the commandant were decorated in the most beautiful style, displaying several transparencies. Dancing was kept up to a late hour when the party retired highly gratified with the unremitting attention of their gallant entertainers, to promote the hilarity of the evening's amusement."[15] In 1841, the officers of the 32nd Foot hosted 200 people at a ball in two rented buildings on Peter Street. As was typical of military festivities, the officers used a variety of weapons to decorate the ballroom: "The walls were completely covered with . . . swords and bayonets, in the shape of stars, &c. A row of bayonets, placed upright, each supporting a wax candle, arranged on a gilt ledge, ran completely around the room, and had a singular beautiful effect. There also were two chandeliers . . . supported by the points of four drawn swords, united at the hilts. The front of the orchestra was one mass of muskets and bayonets and tastefully placed in the shape of a fan, over two highly polished brass drums."[16] Naturally, the unmarried female members of the town's leading families were particular favourites as guests.[17] However, when a budding romance seemed to be heading towards marriage, a young officer might find himself transferred away from York to save him for a more suitable match at a later date if his intended was not socially acceptable to his family back home.[18]

The officers were not the only ones to host social events. Seventy sergeants of the Royal Artillery, and the 32nd and 93rd Regiments "with their wives and sweethearts," celebrated a ball at Mirfield's Inn at the corner of King and York streets in 1840. The party lasted from 7:00 P.M. to 7:00 A.M.[19] Although the officers' parties were open only to their invited guests, drawn mainly from the town's more affluent and powerful families, everyone could enjoy the music presented by regimental bands over the years. In 1833, the band of the 66th Regiment of Foot performed two concerts each week for the public's enjoyment.[20] The members of the garrison also participated in other aspects of the community's social life, such as enjoying cricket, horse racing, and other sporting events.[21] The people of York set their clocks by the sound of the noon gun fired at the fort. The normally reliable signal suddenly became less trustworthy in 1825: "The sun dial at the Garrison west of this city has been eat up by one of His Majesty's Cows – The 12 o'clock gun is therefore fired by guesswork."[22] Everyone in Toronto benefited when the men of the garrison ran to the aid of the civilian population when fires broke out in the town.[23] Sometimes the people of the garrison undertook charitable activities to help the community, as happened in 1844 when the officers of the 82nd Regiment raised a subscription for some poor people in Toronto whose homes had been destroyed by fire.[24]

Pl. 34: Officers of the 83rd Regiment sleighing with their friends on Toronto Bay in the winter of 1842-1843.

Some regiments were more popular with the townspeople than others. The 93rd Foot (Sutherland Highlanders) seems to have been a particular favourite in the late 1830s and early 1840s. A large number of Torontonians were immigrants from Scotland, and the men of the regiment found themselves invited into the homes of many of these people, some of whom were relatives of the soldiers themselves.[25] This regiment also was noted for its "comparative sobriety" and its attendance at a Presbyterian church.[26] (Most regiments used Anglican churches for Sunday worship.)* The editor of one newspaper recorded that he "felt much satisfaction . . . in witnessing the procession of . . . the gallant 93rd . . . to St. Andrew's Church . . . to attend Divine Service, each soldier provided with his Bible. This fine corps . . . has borne a moral as well as a military character second to none in the Service."[27]

Not all relationships were so positive. The presence of a garrison encouraged prostitution and petty crimes, and drunk, disorderly soldiers were a common feature in colonial Toronto. In 1849, for example, soldiers from the Rifle Brigade ambushed and beat up three police officers sent to arrest prostitutes on Garrison Common.[28] Officers as well as the other ranks were a high-spirited group and often offended the sensibilities of the community's sterner citizens. In 1856, a Lieutenant Ord of the 71st Regiment ran up debts with a King Street tobacconist and took too long to settle up with the shopkeeper, a Mr. Lyons. When Lyons went to the garrison to collect, Ord refused to see him and had the guard throw the tobacconist out. Frustrated, Lyons next day purchased a horsewhip and attacked Lieutenant Ord on King Street. The officer survived the attacked reasonably well, but Lyons found himself in court, fined for assault and battery.[29] We do not know if Lyons ever collected his money from Lieutenant Ord. On another occasion, one can imagine the upset experienced by people trying to sleep in the early morning hours of February 16, 1843, when a group of officers – no doubt fortified with drink – amused themselves having "a jovial time going round the town serenading" until daybreak.[30] Other officers and men spent their leisure hours more respectably, such as in attending temperance meetings.[31]

In the decades following the War of 1812, more than just military activities occurred in the garrison. The army relieved the merchants of the town of a major worry by allowing them to store gunpowder in the Stone Magazine.[32] In the 1820s, immigrants to Upper Canada used vacant barracks in Fort York for emergency housing.[33] In 1822, some of these people brought

* The Churches of England and Scotland were the state churches of their respective countries. As such, the army used these denominations for divine worship. The army required Methodists and other Protestants to attend one of the state churches. Roman Catholics in the army attended Roman Catholic services individually. The army allowed members of other faiths, such as Jews, to attend services of their respective religions.

ROYAL ONTARIO MUSEUM, 955.173

Pl. 35: Soldiers were a prominent feature in garrison towns such as Toronto, particularly during the Rebellion Crisis, as shown in this c.1840 painting by John Gillespie of King Street near St. Lawrence Market.

NAC, C-31462

Pl. 36: Canteens, where soldiers could purchase drinks and other consumables, were standard features of the Toronto garrison from the 1790s. Shown here is the canteen at the New Fort in 1887.

smallpox into the garrison, which necessitated moving the sick to Gibraltar Point.[34] In 1840, the first magnetic and meteorological observatory in Canada briefly had its home at the Bathurst Street Barracks, just north of Fort York, under the direction of the Royal Artillery.[35]

Within this long period when the British army garrisoned Toronto after the War of 1812, three events stand out in the fort's history: the Rebellion Crisis of 1837-1841, the "replacement" of Fort York in 1841, and the Trent Affair of 1861-1862.

THE REBELLION CRISIS

There had been political discontent in Upper Canada for many years before the outbreak of the Rebellion of 1837. Some people wanted a more democratic system of government than the colony's constitution allowed. Others opposed the dominance of Upper Canada's government by the province's more affluent and conservative citizens (disparagingly labelled "the Family Compact"). Some saw the reservation of two-sevenths of the land of every township for government and church use as a serious impediment to growth; others opposed the favoured status of some churches (particularly the Church of England) over denominations such as the Methodists and Baptists. Many people had grievances against the way education, road development, and other local issues were handled.

Despite these widespread complaints, reformers suffered defeat in the 1836 provincial election. They lost in large part because of electoral corruption, accusations that the reformers were treasonous, and because the lieutenant-governor, Sir Francis Bond Head, threw his support behind the conservatives. Many people were outraged at Head's actions because they believed the governor should have been politically neutral. Reformers, having lost control of the legislative assembly, organized political unions to pressure the government for reform. Some of the more extreme reformers thought these unions could be turned into a military force to bring about political change.

Towards the autumn of 1837, William Lyon Mackenzie, the principal leader of the radical reformers, decided to overthrow the government, impose an American-style constitution on the colony, and declare independence from Britain.[36] He may even have wanted to have Upper Canada annexed to the United States.[37] By October, Mackenzie began to share some of his thoughts with others and raise support for his coup.[38] At the beginning of December, Mackenzie gathered supporters north of Toronto at Montgomery's Tavern on Yonge Street (just north of today's Eglinton Avenue) in preparation for a surprise attack on the city. Mackenzie planned first to take Toronto, then Fort York.

Mackenzie misled many of his followers by telling them exaggerated tales about government repression and keeping from them his intent to lead an armed rebellion against the govern-

Pl. 37: William Lyon Mackenzie (1795-1861). A native of Scotland, Mackenzie emigrated to Canada in 1820 where he worked variously as a merchant and newspaper publisher. His most famous newspaper, the *Colonial Advocate* was known for its strong condemnation of the provincial government. Elected to the legislative assembly in 1828, he gradually emerged as the leader of the radical reformers. After the rebellion, he lived in exile in the United States until 1850 when he returned to Canada following a pardon granted to him by Queen Victoria.

ment. Many "rebels" later claimed that they had been duped into joining the rebellion, had been threatened if they did not take part, or had been told that anti-government support was more widespread than actually was the case.[39] Many, for example, had been told, falsely, that the government had been overthrown in Lower Canada.[40] One man said he had heard that in Toronto there were huge quantities of firearms that the government was going to "put into the Hands of . . . Indians, Negroes, and Orange Men" to "Murder plunder, Burn and destroy the peaceable Inhabitants" of the province, thus necessitating an armed response.[41]

As Mackenzie marshalled his forces, Fort York sat virtually undefended because Sir Francis Head had sent most of his Upper Canadian garrison to Lower Canada, including 225 men of the 24th Regiment of Foot from Toronto. Head thought there would be no serious uprising in the upper province requiring troops, although he believed the lower province was in danger because French-English animosities intensified the reform-conservative rift. This transfer left only eight members of the Royal Artillery to protect Fort York.[42] These men moved into the security of Blockhouse Number 2 in the centre of the fort to defend both themselves and the military stores housed in that building if attacked. From this citadel, they sent patrols out to safeguard the fort as best they could.[43]

With only a handful of soldiers and a few constables in Toronto, Mackenzie saw the seizure of the lieutenant-governor and the capture of the town and garrison as both easy and profitable tasks. There were thousands of militia muskets stored in the city hall at St. Lawrence Market, as well as the artillery at Fort York, with which he could arm his followers, to say nothing of the vast quantities of gunpowder and other military stores that were ripe for the picking in the garrison.[44] With the capture of Toronto – which Mackenzie himself may have believed might be achieved without bloodshed – Mackenzie planned to establish a provisional government headed by Dr. John Rolph, a respected Toronto reformer.[45] To solidify the rebel hold on the province after the fall of Toronto, Mackenzie intended to send a steamboat full of rebels to Kingston and capture Fort Henry as it too was virtually undefended with the transfer of troops to Lower Canada.[46]

Word of Mackenzie's plans reached the government before the rebels could act, and although officials, particularly Sir Francis Head, foolishly did not take the threat seriously at first, Mackenzie wasted time and lost the opportunity to make a decisive attack at the point when his forces outnumbered government supporters. After some minor skirmishing between loyalists and rebels north of Toronto on December 4, in which one man on each side died – including Mackenzie's one experienced military leader – the governor and his supporters realized that the danger of an uprising was serious. Accordingly, government supporters began to organize Toronto's defences at the eleventh hour.

MTL, T1749

Pl. 38: Sir Francis Bond Head (1793-1875). Before becoming lieutenant-governor of Upper Canada in 1836, Head had been an officer in the Royal Engineers, a manager of a mining enterprise in Argentina, and a poor law commissioner in Kent. He returned to England in disgrace after the Mackenzie Rebellion because of his incompetent handling of the province's affairs.

NAC, C-40831

Pl. 39: The creator of this crude racist cartoon hoped to incite opposition to the government for recruiting Black and Aboriginal peoples to defend the colony during the Rebellion Crisis. For their part, Blacks and Natives believed a successful rebellion would lead to the American annexation of Upper Canada and a corresponding degradation in their already precarious position in the province.

They raised barricades, posted armed civilians in various buildings, and appointed guards to protect the banks.[47]

On December 5, 1837, Mackenzie marched down Yonge Street at the head of between 500 and 700 men. (At that time, Head had only 250 supporters by his side.) Some rebels had firearms, others carried home-made pikes, some had clubs and sticks, but many had no weapons at all. Meanwhile, another 100 to 200 rebels waited inside the city, prepared to spring into action once Mackenzie entered Toronto.[48] In the face of these threats, the government's pickets north of the city (at modern Bloor Street) were called in. Frightened and hoping to defuse the crisis, Sir Francis sent negotiators to Mackenzie to see what the rebels wanted.

At this point, the rebellion began to falter. Head soon learned that the rebel force numbered in the hundreds, not the thousands he had been led to believe was the case. Therefore, he terminated negotiations. Mackenzie, instead of ordering a quick attack on Toronto before Sir Francis could consolidate his position, squandered more time north of the city burning down the house of one of his critics and engaging in other ineffective activities. By the time he resumed his march towards the city, it was late afternoon and many of his frustrated and unwilling supporters had deserted. Meanwhile, the governor's supporters assembled at St. Lawrence Market and at the parliament buildings (between Simcoe and John streets on Front Street), and thirty men formed a picket on Yonge Street to watch the main road into the city from the north.[49]

Near the corner of Yonge and College streets, the picket, led by Sheriff William Jarvis, took cover across the rebels' line of march.[50] At dusk, Mackenzie's men came within range. The sheriff's men opened fire, hit a few rebels, but immediately ran away in terror because they were so badly outnumbered.[51] The rebels shot back, but almost all of them fled up Yonge Street in panic a few moments later. There were no government casualties in this skirmish. One rebel was killed and several were wounded.[52] Soon afterwards, more rebel sympathizers deserted. Exactly why the rebels retreated is unclear. Mackenzie claimed that his men ran because they thought their front ranks had been killed when in fact they fell to the ground after firing only so the rear ranks could fire over their heads. At the same time, a terrifying rumour spread through the rebel ranks that government supporters lined Yonge Street and would subject them to a withering barrage all the way into the city.[53] The very fact that loyal forces opened fire may have convinced many rebels that Mackenzie was wrong to think Toronto could be taken easily. Many of his supporters, while willing to participate in a political demonstration, even a riotous one, simply were not prepared to engage in a deadly revolution.

This setback did not discourage Mackenzie. He decided to launch another attack two days later on December 7 after the ex-

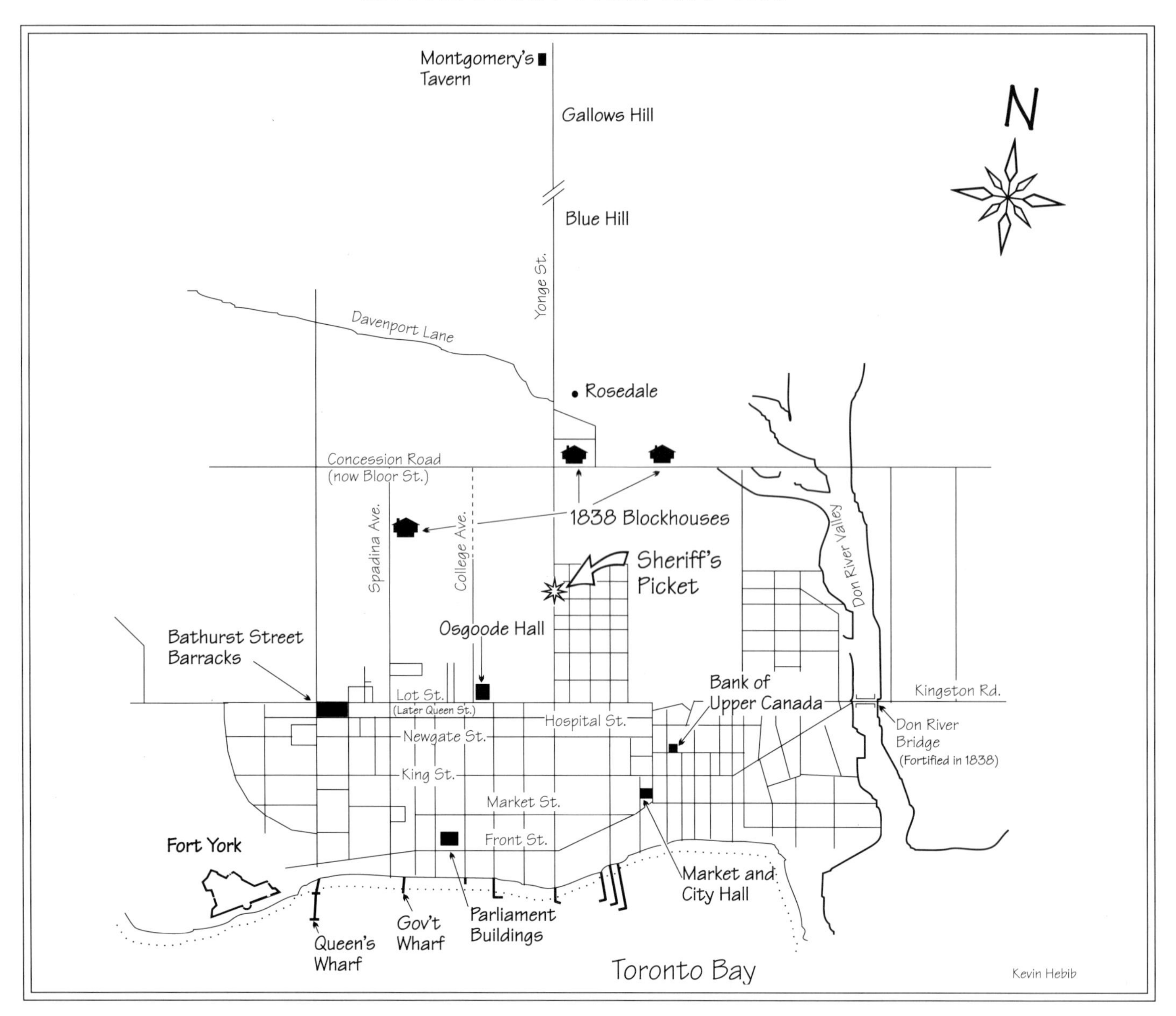

Map 9: Toronto during the Rebellion Crisis.

pected arrival of reinforcements at Montgomery's Tavern. Meanwhile, people loyal to the government converged on the capital to protect the city from the rebels. These people enabled Head to extend his area of control to other critical defensive points in the city, including Fort York.[54] Growing government support led John Rolph and others to advise Mackenzie to call off the uprising and disperse his force – advice that Mackenzie chose to ignore.

On December 6, Mackenzie led forty or fifty of his supporters on a patrol south to Davenport Lane (now Road) and robbed a stagecoach and a tavern.[55] On the government side, Sir Francis sent Cornelia De Grassi (who was about thirteen years old) to perform a reconnaissance of the rebel camp on the pretext of visiting a local shop. It was becoming obvious to both sides that the government was winning the war of numbers as loyal Upper Canadians were rallying faster than rebellious ones. To make matters worse for Mackenzie, his people continued to desert. Growing government strength encouraged Sir Francis Head to take bolder action. The loyalists began arresting rebel supporters in Toronto and prepared a counter-attack for December 7.

On the seventh, Mackenzie ordered Peter Matthews to take sixty men to seize the Montréal stagecoach as it approached Toronto from the east and burn the Don River bridge. Mackenzie hoped this manoeuvre would create a diversion to draw government supporters east from Toronto while he led his main force against the city again. Matthews managed to set fire to the bridge and some neighbouring buildings and skirmished with government supporters. However loyal militiamen and two fire companies from Toronto drove the rebels away, killing one in the process, and put out most of the fires.[56]

Mackenzie's attack, planned to occur at the same time as the Don River raid, never happened. Instead, the lieutenant-governor took the initiative and marched north with 1,200 men in three columns – accompanied by two 6-pounder cannon and two bands of music – to attack the rebel headquarters. Led by a veteran officer of the War of 1812, James Fitzgibbon, the militia attacked Montgomery's Tavern in the early afternoon (then defended by only 450 men, of whom 200 hid from the loyalists rather than fight). Within half an hour of the first shots being fired, Fitzgibbon's columns outflanked and dispersed the rebels and set fire to the tavern. Casualties were light: five government supporters were wounded; one rebel was killed in action and a few were wounded, some of whom later died.[57] Interestingly, Head refused to take either the Royal Artillerymen from Fort York or a couple of regular army officers who were in Toronto with him, believing it was politically better to put down the rebellion with loyal Upper Canadians unsupported by imperial troops.[58]

Once the loyalists dispersed the rebels from Montgomery's Tavern, militiamen pursued and skirmished with fleeing rebels.

Some government supporters looted rebel homes, especially of foodstuffs, which were badly needed in Toronto because Mackenzie had cut the flow of supplies to the city during his short siege.[59] Just after the Montgomery's Tavern action, Sir Francis ordered James Fitzgibbon to burn the home of one of Mackenzie's supporters, David Gibson, which Fitzgibbon reluctantly did. Fitzgibbon was so upset by the impropriety of torching the house that he resigned his position of acting adjutant-general of the militia next day.[60]

Another rising occurred in western Upper Canada that December, but the militia, supported by the Grand River Iroquois, suppressed it with little difficulty. Mackenzie fled to the United States and set up a "provisional government" on Navy Island in the Niagara River, up river from Niagara Falls. In the weeks and months that followed, rebel supporters, joined by American adventurers, launched raids – some quite serious – into Upper Canada at various points along the international border. Harsh treatment of rebels and their sympathizers by both the government and its supporters caused considerable bitterness, raising fears that many Upper Canadians might join any force from the United States that could secure a beach head in the province.

To defend the province from both external and internal threats immediately after the Mackenzie rebellion, the provincial government mustered a number of volunteer companies of militia (such as the "Toronto City Guards") for full-time service. Within days of the Yonge Street skirmishes, several hundred militiamen garrisoned Fort York, while others guarded key points around the city and harbour.[61] By early February 1838, there were 1,950 militiamen serving in Toronto from a variety of new units with such fanciful names as the "Queen's Lancers" and the "Royal Volunteers."[62] The large number of men seems to have exceeded necessity because rebel supporters were completely incapable of attacking the capital in strength. However, the government may have wanted to display its strength to maintain the morale of the population because, as one person noted, there was "a very remarkable want of confidence in the people, especially in Toronto."[63]

Later, mainly because of the threat of raids from the United States, several 550-to-600-man battalions of militia were incorporated (that is, organized, trained, and equipped for full-time service).[64] Towards the end of 1838, the active militia was reorganized again into over thirty volunteer companies and sixteen full battalions: four "incorporated" battalions enrolled for eighteen months' full-time service, and twelve "provisional" battalions enlisted for six months. The 3rd Incorporated and the 2nd and 6th Provisional Battalions had their headquarters in Toronto.[65] To bolster the active militia, the authorities frequently called out both the sedentary militia and the Aboriginal population. Professional backbone for the colonial militia came in the form of 5,000 regular troops dispatched to Upper Canada by the end of

MTL, T10345

Pl. 40: A steamer enters Toronto Bay under the guns of Fort York in 1838, as represented – somewhat fancifully – by Coke Smyth in 1840.

1838.[66] To protect the Great Lakes, several armed steamers were acquired for government service, and a guarded coal-storage facility was built on the government wharf near the military storage buildings east of Fort York to supply fuel to these vessels.[67] Troops in Toronto kept ready for active service through constant drill, which took place behind Fort York in the brush and fields of Garrison Common. Musketry and artillery practice occurred frequently and the entire garrison brigaded together to participate in large-scale manoeuvres twice each week.[68]

Fort York's defences had deteriorated badly after the War of 1812 and needed repairs to make them capable of withstanding attack. Work done in 1838 included repairing the artillery-proof earthworks, enlarging the Circular Battery to hold more cannon, building a firing step along the interior earth wall for the use of infantrymen, and installing a double row of anti-personnel palisades on the exterior face of the earthworks (an upright one at the bottom of the walls and a horizontal one near the top).[69] The army fortified and guarded buildings both inside and outside the fort to protect their occupants from attack.[70] Workmen constructed two vaults in the cellar of the Officers' Brick Barracks to protect from guerrilla raids money belonging to the army and the Bank of Upper Canada.[71] Among other improvements were repairs to barracks, stables, hospitals, and cookhouses, and the conversion of a military storehouse into a prison for rebels. The army also rented accommodation in the city and built new facilities to meet the needs of the greatly increased garrison, including the construction of a large barracks for 330 men in the northwest bastion of the fort.[72]

Around the city, the Royal Engineers fortified the bridge over the Don River and built three blockhouses on the outskirts of Toronto both to protect the city against rebel incursions and to serve as bases for patrols.[73] These blockhouses stood near today's intersections of College Street and Spadina Avenue, Bloor and Sherbourne streets, and Yonge and Bloor streets.[74] According to one officer, the blockhouses gave a "sense of security to the inhabitants" and may have prevented "the very attempts" that they were designed to guard against.[75] These fortifications, along with many of those built in and around Fort York, represented a major shift in Toronto's defensive focus. Except during the Mississauga crisis of the 1790s, defences were planned primarily to protect Toronto against a foreign water-borne attack. While this function remained important – as demonstrated by the improved Circular Battery – the army now had to protect the city against possible raids from disloyal elements of the population. Troops even were stationed in the city itself. The 32nd Regiment of Foot, for example, lived at Osgoode Hall, the New British Coffee House, "Ritchey's" (probably a tavern), and at the new Bathurst Street Barracks built at the southeast corner of Queen and Bathurst streets to accommodate 108 officers and men.[76]

MTL, 977-26-101

Pl. 41: The 1838 Rebellion Barracks as it appeared in the summer of 1928, six years before it was demolished. The 1815 officers' barracks is on the right. (Photograph by Janet A. Hamwood.)

AO, NOTEBOOK AND SKETCHBOOK OF THOMAS GLEGG, 1841-1842

Pl. 42: This sketch shows one of the three blockhouses built in 1838 to protect Toronto against guerrilla raids during the Rebellion Crisis.

Tensions remained high through 1838, 1839, and 1840, but the threat of rebel activity gradually died down with the new decade. The government disbanded all the enroled militia battalions by 1843 except for a small number of men retained for border patrols, including a company of Black soldiers.[77] However, the number of regular troops in Canada increased, not because of the Rebellion Crisis, but because of a renewed threat of war with the United States over the New Brunswick-Maine boundary. By 1842, there were 12,452 regulars in Canada East and West (as Lower and Upper Canada had been renamed in 1841 following their political union into one Province of Canada).[78] However, with the signing of the Webster-Ashburton Treaty,* international tensions eased and most of the extra troops withdrew, only to return when the Oregon Boundary Dispute in the latter part of the 1840s again led to the reinforcement of the Canadian garrison.[79] As the 1840s passed, many of the grievances that had led to rebellion were

* The Webster-Ashburton Treaty had an adverse effect on Canadian defence. In granting the Americans a large portion of the disputed territory, it made communications between the Maritime colonies and Canada more difficult. As the Port of Québec froze during the winter, troops arriving in an emergency during cold weather would have to land at Halifax or Saint John and make a difficult overland march to Québec until later in the century when a railway was built. But, without a long northward detour, a railway also would be exposed to American attack.

NAC, C-2801

Pl. 43: "Pier & Fort, Toronto," 1839, by John Philip Bainbrigge.

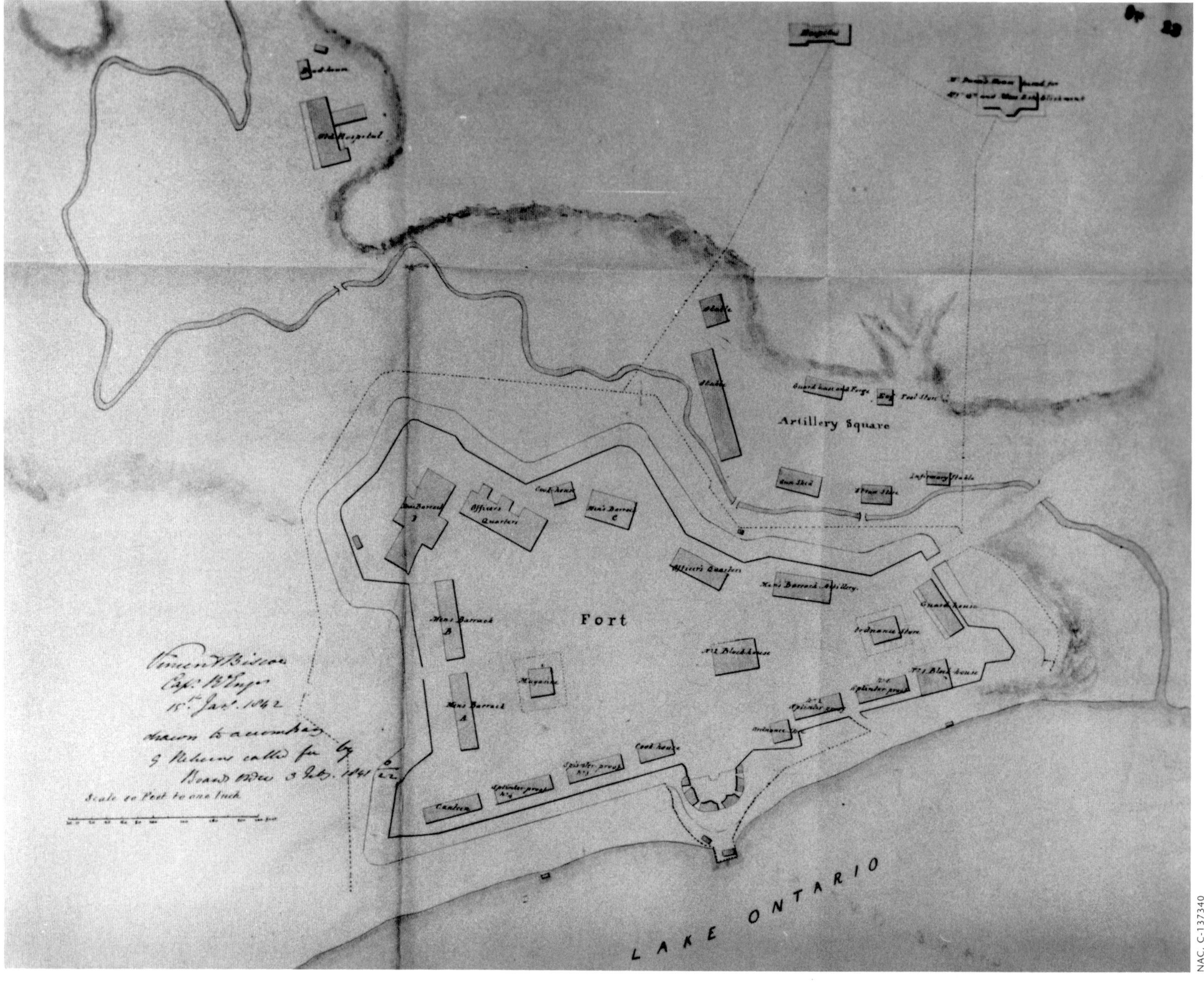
Artillery Square
Stable
Officers Quarters
Mens Barrack C
Cook house
Fort
Mens Barrack B
Mens Barrack A
Magazine
Officers Quarters
Mens Barrack Artillery
Guard house
Ordnance Store
No 2 Blockhouse
No 1 Block house
Splinter proof
Ordnance Store
Canteen
LAKE ONTARIO

NAC, C-137340

resolved through political and democratic means.* By the late 1840s, the Province of Canada had achieved "responsible government" with a cabinet responsible to the elected lower house and a governor who acted according to the wishes of the local parliament.

FORT YORK "REPLACED"

There had been attempts to replace Fort York with better defences and barracks from at least the early 1820s. Part of the motivation stemmed from the rapid deterioration of Fort York after the War of 1812. By 1826, one report described the garrison as a "very ruinous old fort." Most of its buildings were "out of repair," and its vermin-infested wood buildings – considered to have been built as temporary structures during the war – were dismissed as virtually uninhabitable. The outlying fortifications, such as the blockhouse on Gibraltar Point, had largely fallen into ruin.[80]

In 1826, Sir James Carmichael Smyth of the Royal Engineers recommended that Fort York be replaced with a "large and substantial Earthen Redoubt . . . having a fortified [masonry] Keep within it, similar to that of Fort Wellington in the Netherlands."[81] That fort, designed to house 250 men and mount forty-six cannon, had been built outside Ostend during the Napoleonic Wars.[82] It consisted of a central fortified pentagonal tower, surrounded by a deep ditch and strong outerworks. Such a defence would have been far stronger than the existing fort without requiring any more troops than the number normally assigned to York. It also would have addressed another problem raised over the years: that Fort York was only a harbour defence and did not protect the town against attack along Dundas Street or any other inland route.[83] As Upper Canada emerged from the early days of settlement in the second quarter of the nineteenth century, and as roads improved, the Americans would not have been as dependent upon water transportation to get to Toronto as they had been during the War of 1812, thus reducing Fort York's capacity to defend Toronto. With a Fort Wellington-style work, York could be taken only through a time-consuming siege no matter how the Americans got to the town. It was hoped that the garrison could hold out until reinforcements arrived, whereas Fort York might not be defensible for long against a well-equipped and de-

* In popular history, the Rebellion of 1837 has been interpreted as an important step in the development of more democratic government in Upper Canada. However, modern historians generally dispute this, making the point that the Colonial Office had been moving to a more conciliatory policy before the rebellion, but the revolt probably retarded the establishment of responsible government because the British government was nervous about devolving power too quickly to colonies in which some citizens had rebelled so recently. Nova Scotia, which had no rebellion, achieved responsible government before Canada.

Map 10: Fort York in 1842 at the end of the Rebellion Crisis. Note the additional palisading (dotted line) and the enlarged circular battery.

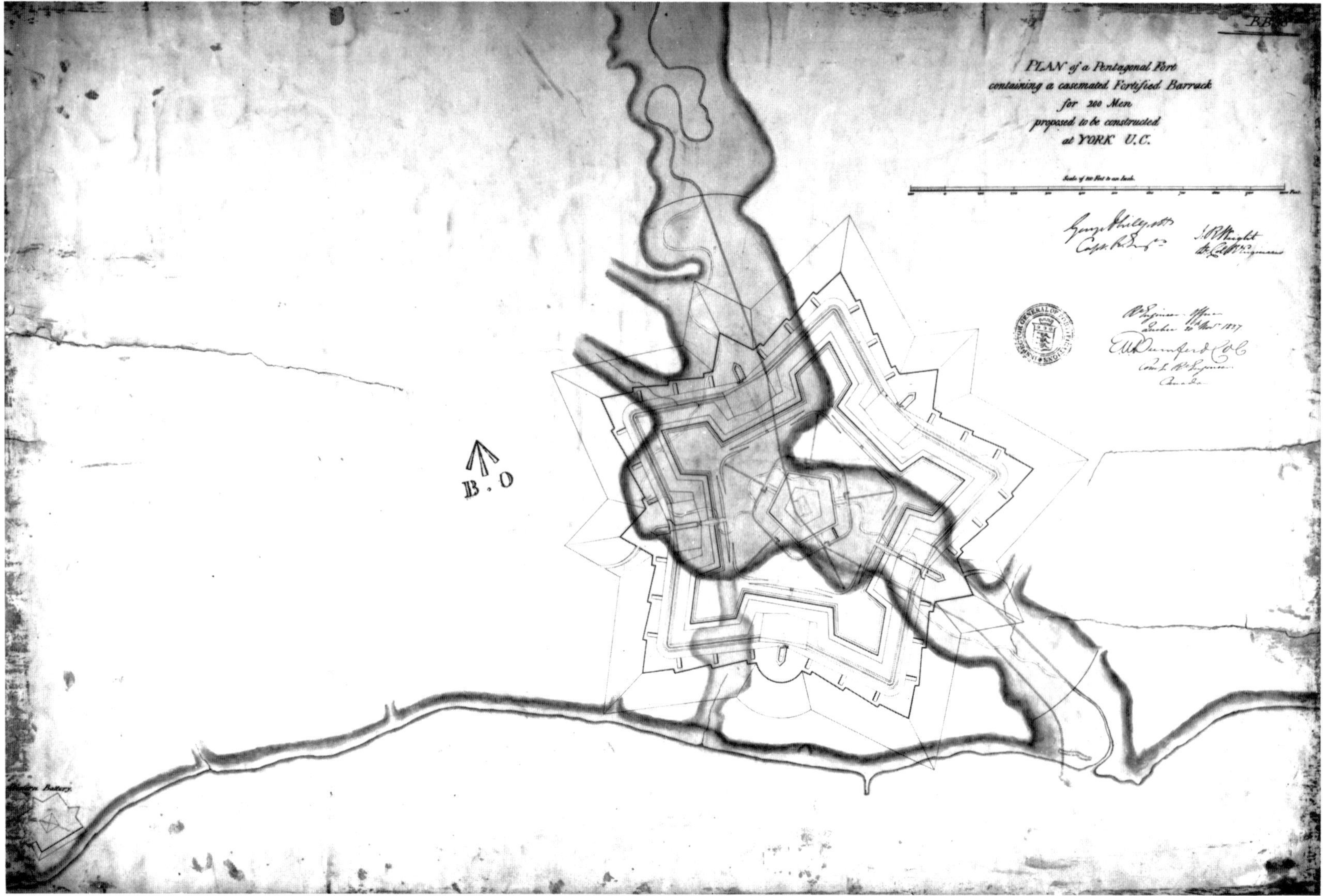

NAC, NMC-23140

Map 11: This 1827 plan shows the proposed fortifications for York following the model of Fort Wellington near Ostend. A new Western Battery with a stone defensive tower (visible on the left of the plan) were to be constructed as well.

NAC, NMC-16817

Map 12: This detail of an 1833 plan of the harbour (south is "up") shows Sir John Colborne's proposed defences for York to the west (right) of Fort York. Note also the Queen's Wharf, the location of one of the proposed Martellos south of the fort, and the narrowness of the navigable part of the channel.

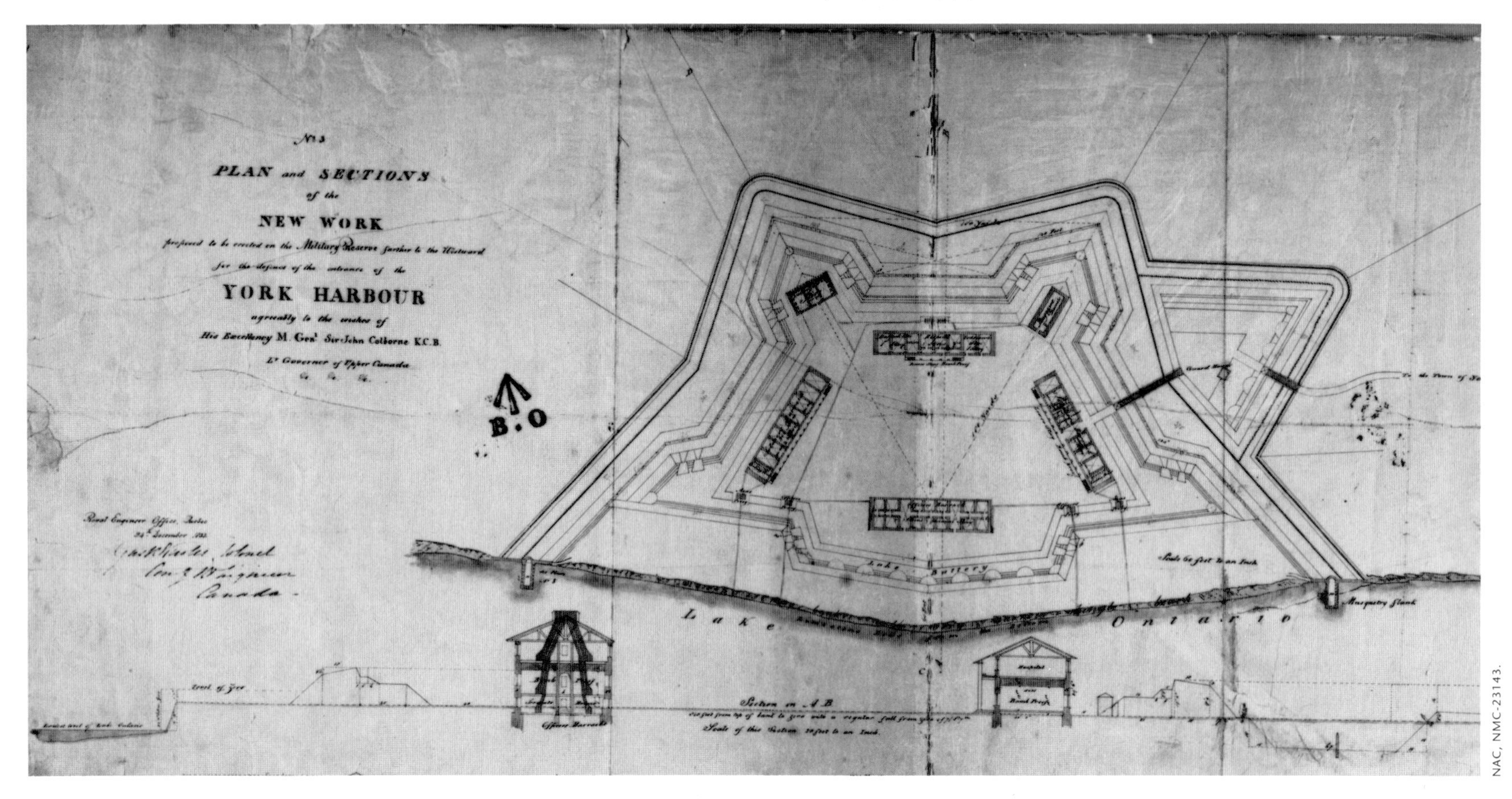

NAC, NMC-23143.

Map 13: This detail shows Colborne's proposed fort. Note the profile on the bottom section.

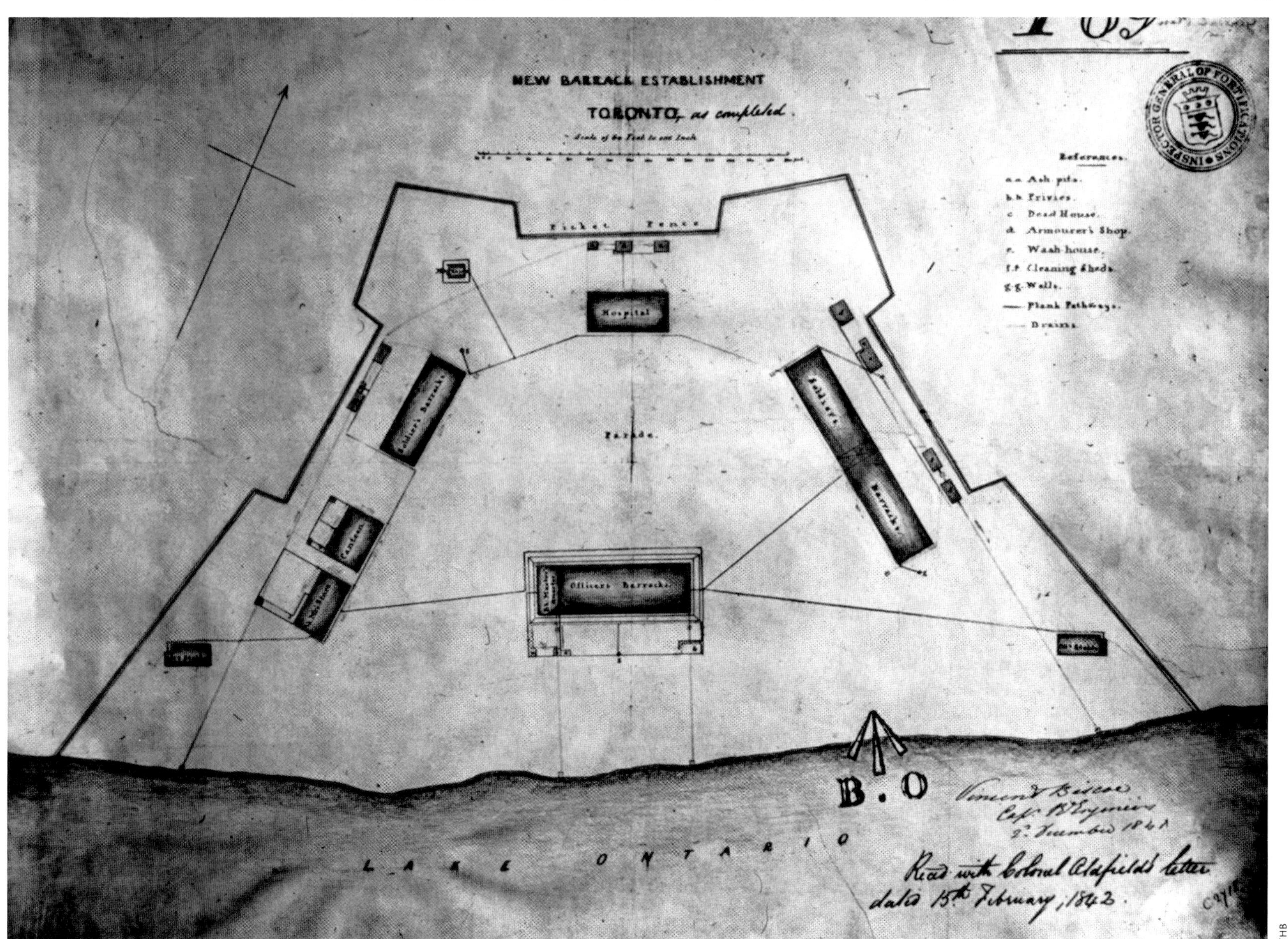

THB

Map 14: The New Fort as built by 1842: barracks with no fortifications except for a palisade or stockade.

NAC, JOHN BOYD COLLECTION, 60874

Pl. 44: The 1841 buildings of the New Fort from a 1913 photograph.

termined enemy.[84] Royal Engineers drew plans for the new fort at the same time the army reduced the maintenance budget for the existing buildings in anticipation of tearing down the old fort.[85] In the end, however, the army decided not to build a Fort Wellington style citadel.

By the early 1830s, the shifting of the sand bar at the harbour entrance seemed to make a site one kilometre west of Fort York a better spot than the old fort for a battery to stop enemy ships from entering the harbour.[86] In 1833, Lieutenant-Governor Sir John Colborne suggested building fortifications just west of the old Western Battery. His plans were different from the Fort Wellington model, but were impressive nevertheless. Colborne's new fort was to consist of a parade square surrounded by stone buildings and defended by a strong bastioned stone and earth wall mounting heavy artillery. To supplement this work, he suggested that a battery be established on the new Queen's Wharf, which was to extend 215 metres south into the harbour from a site just east of Fort York at the foot of Bathurst Street.* [87] On the peninsula side of the harbour entrance, Colborne wanted to build three Martello Towers. One was to be located on the site of the old Gibraltar Point blockhouse. The other two were to be placed in the shallow waters off Gibraltar Point: one 825 metres southwest of the point, where it could cover both the south side of the peninsula and the harbour entrance; the other between the point and Fort York, 825 metres from the former, 750 metres from the latter.[88]

Both Smyth's and Colborne's proposals were doomed by their expense. As it was, military construction elsewhere in Upper Canada far exceeded estimates, a concern that undoubtedly had a negative influence on plans for York. The Rideau Canal, for example, cost £1,134,000 instead of the £169,000 originally estimated.[89] Since York had a modest role in the overall defence of the colony, no extensive defences were erected at that time.[90]

Despite the reluctance to build new fortifications at Toronto, there was agreement that the barrack accommodation at Fort York was substandard and had to be replaced. Therefore, the army implemented Colborne's plan, without the defences, by constructing stone barracks west of Fort York. To finance the project, the army sold a large part of the military reserve east of Fort York. Originally, the reserve was a 400-hectare parcel of land encompassing the ground extending north from Lake Ontario to Queen Street, between Dufferin and Peter streets. The sale of the garrison lands also aided urban growth by allowing the expansion of the city westwards.[91] Despite the sale, construction did not begin until the Rebellion Crisis.[92] The "New Fort" was built of Queenston limestone for £19,000 between February 1840 and October 1841.[93] The only security for the fort was a 2.4-metre-

* The wharf, built in 1833, had no guns placed on it. In wartime, however, it would have been an easy task to arm it.

PRIVATE COLLECTION, COURTESY OF THE ART GALLERY OF ONTARIO WITH PERMISSION OF LAWRENCE FINE ART OF CREWKERNE

Pl. 45: This 1842 watercolour by Henry Bowyer Lane shows the Old Fort and the Queen's Wharf in the foreground, and the New Fort in the background.

high wooden palisade surrounding its perimeter.[94] In 1893, the Canadian government renamed the New Fort "Stanley Barracks" in honour of the governor-general, Lord Stanley of Preston. The New Fort replaced Fort York as the principal barracks for the Toronto garrison until the late 1940s when the Canadian army abandoned the newer site.

Soldiers from the New Fort rushed into Toronto in 1849 during the last violent spasm of the 1837 Rebellion to suppress riots that had broken out over the Rebellion Losses Bill. A reform government had introduced the bill into the Canadian parliament to provide compensation to both government and rebel sympathizers for losses suffered during the Lower Canadian Rebellion. (Upper Canadians already had been compensated.) Conservative elements in Canadian society were outraged when the governor-general, Lord Elgin, gave royal assent to the bill. Many conservatives rioted in Canadian cities, including Toronto, and burned the parliament buildings in Montréal.

Aiding the civil powers in overpowering rioters was the duty the military hated most, but it was necessary because local police forces were too small to deal with mob violence. Most riots were associated with elections and political controversies, indicating how passionately Canadians felt about their politics in the nineteenth century. Troops had to suppress a riot between rival factions after the 1841 municipal election in Toronto.[95] In 1851, magistrates called out the military to put down another riot that erupted as a result of arguments over the clergy reserves.* [96] As late as 1906, soldiers from the New Fort rushed to Hamilton to quell violence during a strike by streetcar operators in that city.[97]

THE TRENT AFFAIR

The army did not abandon Fort York after the construction of the New Fort in 1841. The "Old Fort" continued to have value as both an auxiliary facility for the Toronto garrison and as a harbour defence.

Despite the decision not to fortify the New Fort in 1840-1841, military planners continued to make recommendations for improved harbour defences throughout the 1840s and the 1850s because of Toronto's potential wartime role as a secondary naval base and as a place to protect the Niagara Peninsula and the Toronto Passage.[98] During those decades, officers debated which of

* The clergy reserves were lands that had been set aside by the crown in 1791 to provide an income for the "Established Church," which most people interpreted as meaning the Church of England, although others assumed the term included the Church of Scotland. Many people objected to the clergy reserves for two primary reasons. One was opposition to giving favoured status to one denomination over another, especially since Anglicanism and Presbyterianism were minority faiths in Upper Canada. The other centred on people's unhappiness with the inconveniences caused by having undeveloped church lands within settled regions.

the old and new forts was a better location for a harbour battery. In 1854, the Royal Engineers argued that Fort York was superior. It was higher above the lake – eight metres rather than five – and attacking steamships from the west could be fired on for a considerable time from Fort York before they could steam abreast of it to return fire. Once near the fort and under point-blank fire, enemy vessels likely would be forced onto the sand bar opposite the narrow channel south of Fort York where they could be destroyed easily. In contrast, the New Fort was more vulnerable to a naval barrage and did not block the harbour entrance as effectively as the Old Fort.[99]

The defences recommended for Fort York during those decades included a heavy artillery battery capable of delivering concentrated fire west and south, plus a Martello Tower and some landward defences. An additional gun emplacement was proposed between the old and new forts at either a fuel yard or the old Western Battery site. The Royal Engineers also recommended the construction of batteries at the Humber River and Don River valleys to stop an enemy wanting to attack Toronto overland from the east or west.[100] In 1856, there were plans to sink old ships in the narrow harbour channel if an attack occurred to prevent enemy vessels from getting past Fort York. To stop an American squadron from taking up a position on the south side of the Peninsula and shelling the city from long range with modern artillery, military planners hoped to build field works and either a Martello Tower or a floating battery on the south side of the Peninsula.[101] Nevertheless, no new defences were built until the "Trent Affair" of 1861, during the American Civil War, created a panic that led to the re-armament of Fort York's harbour defences.

On November 8, 1861, the USS *San Jacinto* stopped the British steamship *Trent* on the Atlantic Ocean and forcibly removed two Confederate diplomats. With this incident, which magnified existing tensions with the United States, British North America was put on a war footing. The colonial governments increased the capabilities of their militias and reinforcements sailed from elsewhere in the Empire to bolster the North American garrison, including 1,200 regulars dispatched to Toronto. Many of these troops had to be housed at Fort York, the parliament buildings, and rented accommodation because there was not enough room for them at the New Fort.[102]

The army rebuilt Fort York's defensive walls, installed seven 8-inch shell guns along the south face of the fort, constructed a new Western Battery, and mounted a pair of 32-pounder cannon behind its defences.[103] To hone the skills of the artillerists, the army purchased floating targets in 1862.[104] In the end, these guns were not needed as the Trent Affair passed without recourse to arms, largely because of the intervention of Queen Victoria's husband, Prince Albert, in the diplomatic exchanges between Britain and the United States.

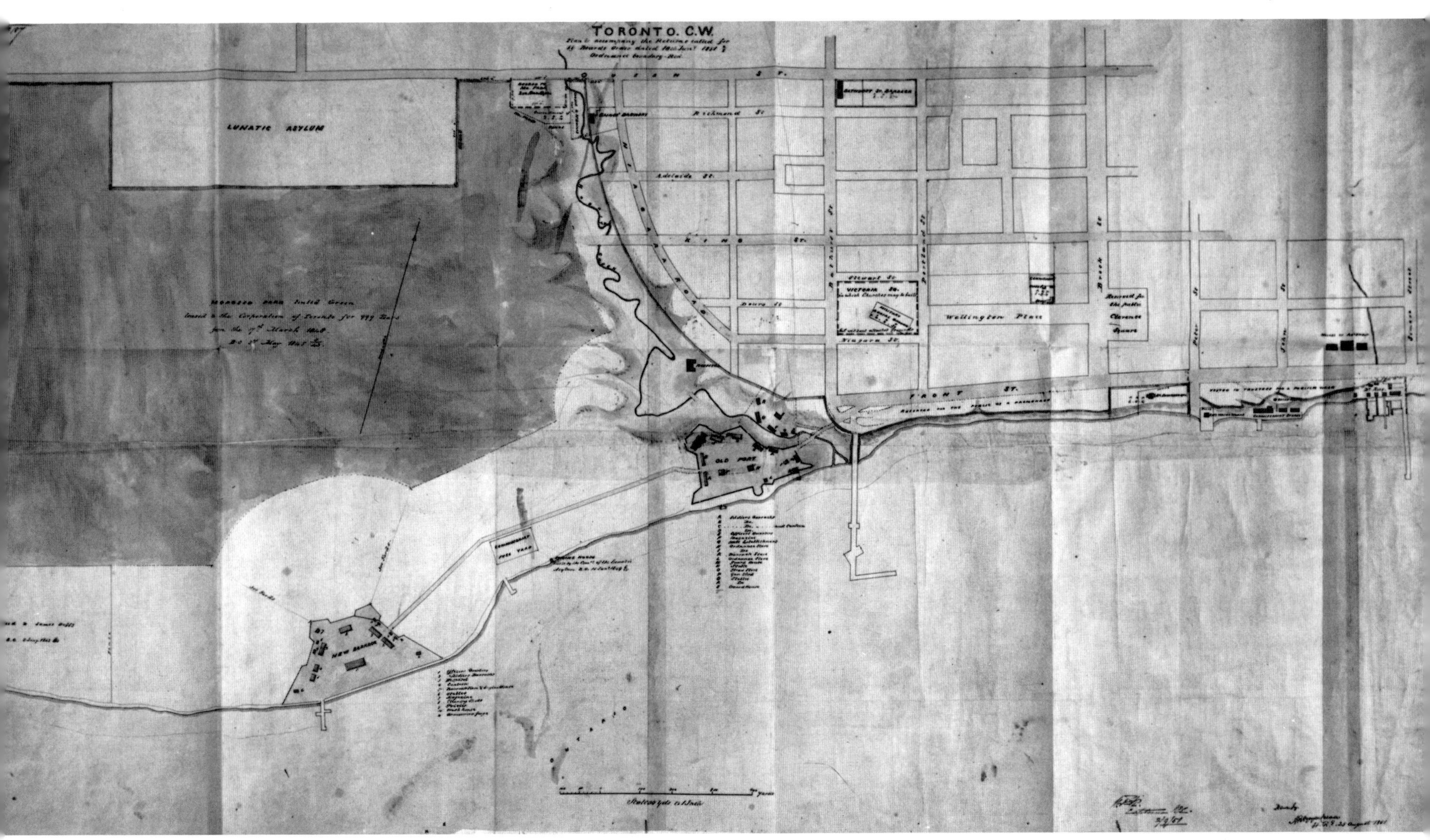

NAC, C-137339

Map 15: The Old Fort and New Fort (on the right and left respectively) in 1851. East of Fort York, along Front Street, are commissariat warehouses. The garrison cemetery of 1793-1860 is just northeast of Fort York, and the Bathurst Street Barracks can be seen north of the cemetery at the corner of Bathurst and Queen Streets.

Pl. 46: Fort York from the east in 1860 from an engraving by Benson J. Lossing.

CANADIAN FORCES ASSUME RESPONSIBILITY FOR FORT YORK

Canadians served at Fort York from its earliest days, as recruits in the British regiments stationed in York, as militia serving on garrison duty, and in regiments recruited in the British North American colonies, such as the Canadian Fencibles of the War of 1812 era. But in all these cases, primary responsibility for Toronto's defence lay with the British army, whose officers were responsible to the British government even if the officers themselves were Canadians. This was a logical situation given the primitive state of colonial society in the late eighteenth and early nineteenth centuries. As British North America became more populous and wealthy, and as Canadians assumed greater political control over their affairs, the issue of how much responsibility Canadians should take for their defence became a source of controversy when the British government attempted to transfer responsibility for local military affairs to reluctant colonial governments.

At the time of the Crimean War in the 1850s, the imperial government withdrew the entire British garrison in Toronto temporarily, and, for the first time, Canadian authorities assumed primary responsibility for Toronto's defences for a period of two years. The province enlisted 150 "enroled pensioners" who had been given land grants on military property when they retired from the British army on condition they held themselves in readiness to serve if required. Their numbers were too small to act as a military force of any consequence, but they were useful in maintaining forts for use by the militia should an emergency occur and as a supplement to the police in times of riot or civil disorder.[105]

At the same time, the provincial government commissioned a study to examine the colony's broader defensive requirements. The commission recommended re-organizing the old sedentary militia which, while comprising the bulk of the male population, had little training or equipment. In addition, the commission proposed that a part-time force of better-trained volunteer regiments be created and that weapons, uniforms, and equipment be purchased to outfit a force of 100,000 soldiers.[106] This was the first time Canadians took an interest in their own defence when the colony was not immediately threatened by foreign invasion or insurrection. Much of this concern stemmed from Canadian enthusiasm to help Britain in the patriotic mood of the Crimean War. In response to new colonial concerns for defence, the British government transferred the military lands of Toronto and forty-two other posts to the Province of Canada.[107] Nonetheless, the imperial government thought it necessary to reinforce Canada with its own troops again in 1856 because of a worrisome deterioration of Anglo-American relations and increased American talk of annexing the British colonies.[108]

Some people in Britain opposed sending large numbers of men to North America because they believed such an action would take the incentive away from Canadians to accept responsibility for their own defence.[109] This fear seems to have been justified as interest in military affairs waned by the late 1850s. Most Canadians thought that a large defence establishment was not required in peacetime because the militia could be assembled *en masse* quickly to meet any crisis. Nineteenth-century Canadians enjoyed a myth that held that the Americans had been defeated in the War of 1812 by the local militia – a myth that was false in so far as it did not recognize the central role of professional troops, to say nothing of the Aboriginal peoples, in defending Upper and Lower Canada.

Yet, for a time, the progress of the American Civil War of 1861-1865 undermined confidence in the militia myth and forced British North Americans to reconsider their defensive needs. Despite their opposition to slavery, the British and Canadians generally favoured the southern, or Confederate, side in the war. By about 1863, when it seemed probable that the northern, or Union side, would win, people began to think the Americans might turn their massive armies against the British provinces as soon as they defeated the Confederacy. During these years, the American government upgraded fortifications on its side of the international border, and several incidents occurred in the Great Lakes region that increased tensions between Britain and the United States. At the same time, some American politicians called for the annexation of Canada through military conquest. In February 1865, Canadians were shocked to learn that the Union and Confederate sides were discussing a proposal to end the Civil War by going to war as allies against a third power in defence of the Monroe Doctrine (an American declaration that rejected European claims to sovereignty in the western hemisphere). The third party the Americans had in mind was France in Mexico, not Britain in Canada, but these negotiations caused considerable dismay in both the United Kingdom and British North America.[110] Unease increased in Canada with the activities of the Fenian Brotherhood, a secret society of Irish nationalists that organized border raids in 1866, 1870, and 1871 from the United States to strike blows for Irish independence.[111] In the 1866 raid of the Niagara Peninsula, the British garrison in Toronto and the city's volunteer regiments rushed to the "front" near Fort Erie while less trained rural and small-town militia companies descended on the city to protect it from Fenian sympathizers within Toronto's Irish Catholic community.[112]

Viewing the prospect of war with the United States, many Canadians realized that peacetime defence spending was necessary because fortifications, canals, and the other capital resources required to defend British North America could not be built fast enough to meet the challenge of a large-scale invasion.[113] In some ways, Canadians had been shocked into this conclusion because the British government increasingly came to believe that the

MTL, T11637

Pl. 47: This 1885 photograph of the east end of the fort shows the rotting remains of the palisades towards the top of the earthworks that had been installed in the 1860s. Palisades could stop or slow an assault but, because there was a gap between each log, could not be used by an enemy for cover.

Pl. 48: The Queen's Own Rifles, a volunteer militia regiment, as it appeared about the time of the Fenian Raids.

territory west of Montréal was indefensible against the huge armies the United States had created during the Civil War. The British simply were not willing to throw away troops by placing soldiers in small garrisons in a hopeless defence of the colonies, so the imperial authorities wanted to concentrate their troops only in strong points such as Halifax and Québec.[114] Yet with a greater Canadian commitment to defence, particularly from 1864 onwards, some military strategists claimed that only the land west of Hamilton would have to be forfeited early in a war if the old Kingston naval base were re-established, and if new fortifications were built at Toronto or Hamilton (providing, of course, that the St. Lawrence River could be defended).[115] If a slow fighting withdrawal from Canada West could be combined with a strong defence of Canada East, in addition to vigorous counterattacks against the American Atlantic coast from bases in the Atlantic provinces, Bermuda, and the West Indies, these strategists thought peace negotiations would enable the British to regain any lost territory.

During this tense period, Lieutenant-Colonel William F. Drummond Jervois of the Royal Engineers prepared a secret report on colonial defence. He wrote that strong fortifications were needed because British and Canadian forces would be outnumbered badly in a war. Therefore, they probably would not be able to take on the Americans in large open-field battles, but would have to rely on fortifications to defend the colony.[116] If strong enough, these forts might hold out through a campaigning season until cold weather forced the Americans to lift their sieges. By holding out, the local defenders could buy valuable time for troops to be sent from Britain both to reinforce Canada and to attack the American coastal states.[117]

Jervois recommended that either London, Hamilton, or Toronto be fortified for the defence of Canada West. He seems to have suggested three choices in order to garner support from politicians representing the different communities for the re-fortification of the province, with the hard choice of a particular location to be determined after the easier decision to re-fortify had been made. Of the three, Toronto seemed to have been the most desirable location in his thinking.[118] Jervois saw a re-fortified Toronto as admirably suited as a secondary naval base to Kingston, as a rallying point for troops, and as the gateway to protecting the upper lakes along the route of the old Toronto Passage – attitudes comparable to those of Simcoe seventy years earlier. Unlike the backwoods York of the 1790s, however, the Toronto of the 1860s was a major urban centre capable of providing a great many needs of a military force and was the hub of an important railway network with good communications to other strategic points.

Jervois recommended the construction of both landward and harbour defences for Toronto. On the landward side, he suggested extensive earthworks and batteries be built between the Don and

MTL, T30704

Pl. 49: HMS *Heron*, photographed in Toronto Harbour at Confederation, was one of the *Britomart* class of gunboats which cruised the Great Lakes during the tense 1860s. Propelled by a mix of steam and sail, the *Heron* boasted design improvements informed by the Crimean War experiences of earlier gunboat models.

(Facing page) Map 16: Colonel Jervois's plans for the fortification of Toronto included the construction of two Martello Towers on the island, batteries at the New Fort, and extensive earthworks around the city.

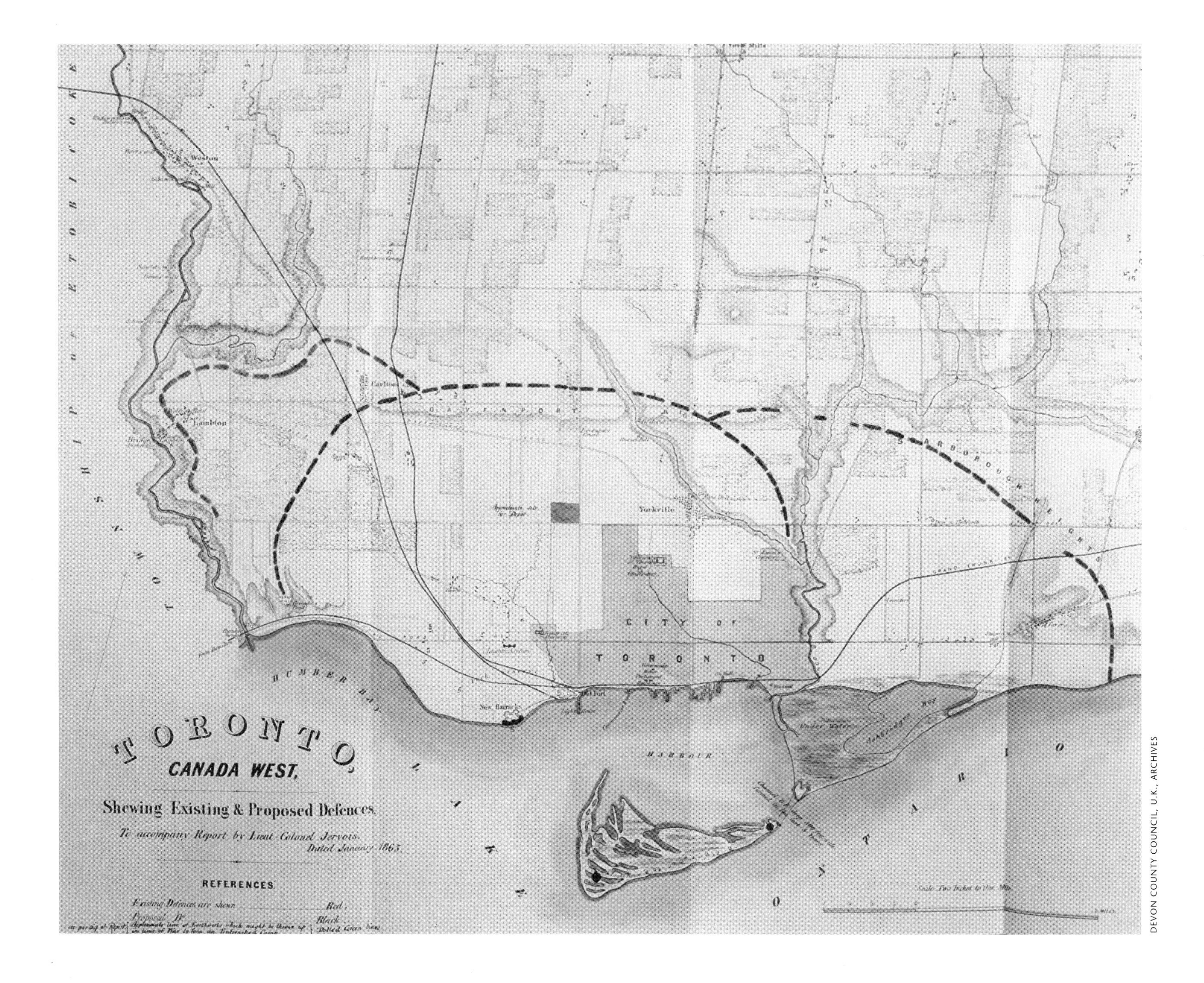

DEVON COUNTY COUNCIL, U.K., ARCHIVES

COURTESY OF THE DIRECTOR, NATIONAL ARMY MUSEUM, LONDON

Pl. 50: This 1865 watercolour shows the battery and palisades installed during the Trent Affair. Note the railway line south of the fort on new lake fill. The large building in the background is the Rebellion Barracks.

Humber rivers along the height of land north of Davenport Road to protect the northern approach. The eastern and western approaches were to be guarded by batteries and other works along these two river valleys as well as with additional fortifications along Scarborough Heights.[119] To defend the harbour, he proposed that two Martello Towers be constructed on the island, one at the east end and one on the south, as well as a battery at the New Fort and batteries near the mouths of the Humber and Don rivers. (The tower on the east end of the peninsula was necessary because a gap had been created in the eastern section of the peninsula in the late 1850s. This gap began to be used as an alternative harbour entrance and eventually became a proper channel in the late nineteenth century.) With the new works, Jervois thought Fort York could be demolished since he disagreed with the military planners of the previous decade who claimed that Fort York was better suited for a shore battery than the New Fort.[120] Jervois believed that the armaments for these defensive works should include the new, heavy, rifled artillery then coming into use, which were capable of piercing the recently developed armour-plated warships of the 1860s. He proposed to mount these guns on field carriages so they could be moved easily to meet whatever emergency Toronto's defenders had to face, unlike the immobile Trent Affair guns mounted on garrison carriages at Fort York.* [121]

In the end, these defences were never constructed. The American threat declined following the disbandment of most of the United States Army after the Civil War and the return of more normal Anglo-American relations. Toronto, therefore, remained dependent primarily upon Fort York's old deteriorating defences in an age of rapid advancements in military technology. One writer described Toronto's defences with these unflattering words: "The barracks are surrounded by an earthen parapet, provided with traverses and embrasures, and there is a very quaint and fantastic earthen redoubt on the beach [the Western Battery], but any ordinary vessel of war could lay the whole establishment in ruins with perfect impunity in half an hour."[122] Although these were exaggerated comments designed to frighten British and Canadian authorities into re-fortifying Canada, they

* For harbour defences, Jervois wrote: "For the defence of Lake Ontario, considering the nature of vessels to which they would be opposed, 68-pounders [31 kg] and 8-inch [20.3 cm] shell guns might, at all events in the first instance, form the main portion of the armament. There should, however, be some 70-pounder [32 kg] rifled guns for long range, as also a few powerful pieces of ordnance which would do effective damage to the armoured portion of iron-plated gun boats." For landward defences, he suggested: "A portion should consist of 40-pounder [18 kg] rifle guns, or other ordnance of about that size, mounted on travelling carriages, so that they might be easily withdrawn if necessary; and that, if desired, a great number of guns might be concentrated on any point. There should also be some heavier pieces of ordnance, both rifled and smooth bore, to bear on the enemy's trenches in the event of siege. . . . Much of the armament for the land works might, perhaps, consist of [older] guns, which since the introduction of armour-plated ships, are no longer applicable for coast fortifications."

Pl. 51: In anticipation of hostilities, the American army refortified its closest post to Toronto, Fort Niagara, between 1863 and 1872. Shown in this 1926 photograph are the masonry landward defences begun during the American Civil War.

nevertheless pointed out that Toronto was not well-defended. He was wrong, however, to be so critical of the defensive walls being earth. The experience of the American Civil War demonstrated that earthworks were better able to withstand bombardment by the artillery of the period than the stone or brick walls that had been so popular in fortification construction in the mid-nineteenth century.[123]

In 1867, Nova Scotia, New Brunswick, and the United Province of Canada confederated to form a country within the British Empire, the Dominion of Canada. (Canada West became Ontario; Canada East became Québec.) In 1868, the dominion purchased the vast northern interior of the continent from the Hudson Bay Company. British Columbia and Prince Edward Island joined Confederation in 1871 and 1873 respectively. (Newfoundland did not join until 1949.) Although Canadians were not willing to devote significant resources to a standing army, part of the motivation for Confederation was a belief that the combined militias of the British North American provinces could withstand American annexation attempts better if they were united under one central authority. As well as not being willing to maintain a large regular army, the Canadian government chose not to spend money on extensive fortifications, but instead invested in a transcontinental railway. The railway, through the east-west economic and social links it created, probably did more to save the Canadian west from American annexation than any military defence could have done.

THB

Pl. 52: Members of the Toronto Field Battery at Fort York took a break from training to pose with their 9-pounder muzzle loading rifles in 1878. The photograph also shows a pile of well-maintained cannon balls for use in the Trent Affair guns. The guns were located approximately where the photographer stood when he took this photograph.

In 1870, the British government withdrew its forces from all secondary North American garrisons such as Toronto and returned these posts, along with primary responsibility for local defence, to the new Canadian federal government.* The formal return of the Toronto barracks occurred on July 25, 1870, with the actual transfer being completed by the end of September.[124] Before the British army left, however, men of Toronto's last imperial garrison travelled west to Manitoba to suppress the Red River Rebellion, accompanied by two volunteer militia battalions that had received their training at the Old and New Forts. In keeping with the transfer of defensive responsibility to Canada, the British troops formed only one-third of this initial expeditionary force.[125] In 1871 and 1872, reinforcements for the Manitoba garrison came exclusively from Canadian militia volunteers who received advanced training in Toronto before heading west.[126] Later, in 1873, the federal government formed the North West Mounted Police to bring law and order to the west and to assert Canadian sovereignty on the prairies against possible American threats. The first recruits assembled and trained at the New Fort before beginning their westward journey.[127]

In 1871, the government created a very small regular Canadian army or "Permanent Force" consisting largely of former British troops, and in 1872 its first detachments arrived in Toronto to take responsibility for the city's military works, which had not been maintained properly by the militia. As might be expected to have occurred in the two years between the withdrawal of the British regulars and the arrival of their Canadian counterparts, the detachment's commander, Sam B. Steele, found "everything in the worst state of confusion, disorder, and neglect."[128] Within a month, Steele restored order and his regulars began to fulfil their primary responsibility of training the local militia since the permanent force simply was too small to defend the country.[129] Not all Canadians were happy to place their confidence in a small permanent force backed up by a large militia. Lieutenant-Colonel Robert Davies, for example, wrote in 1873 that Canada had no choice but to maintain a large professional army, a powerful fleet of gunboats, and a large reserve force because the United States was a "grasping, covetous tyrant, and if we want to look upon ourselves as reasonably well insured, we must keep up a good fighting establishment, not only to secure our liberties, but because the knowledge of such a fact actually lessens the danger of war"![130]

From the arrival of the first Canadian regulars until the early 1930s when Fort York became a historic site museum, the fort served as part of the Canadian army's Toronto post. Most of the troops lived and worked at the New Fort but Fort York fulfilled secondary roles as married quarters for the regulars, militia of-

* The British maintained garrisons after 1870 only at Halifax, Nova Scotia, and Esquimalt, British Columbia. The last imperial troops to leave the rest of Canada departed Québec City in November 1871.

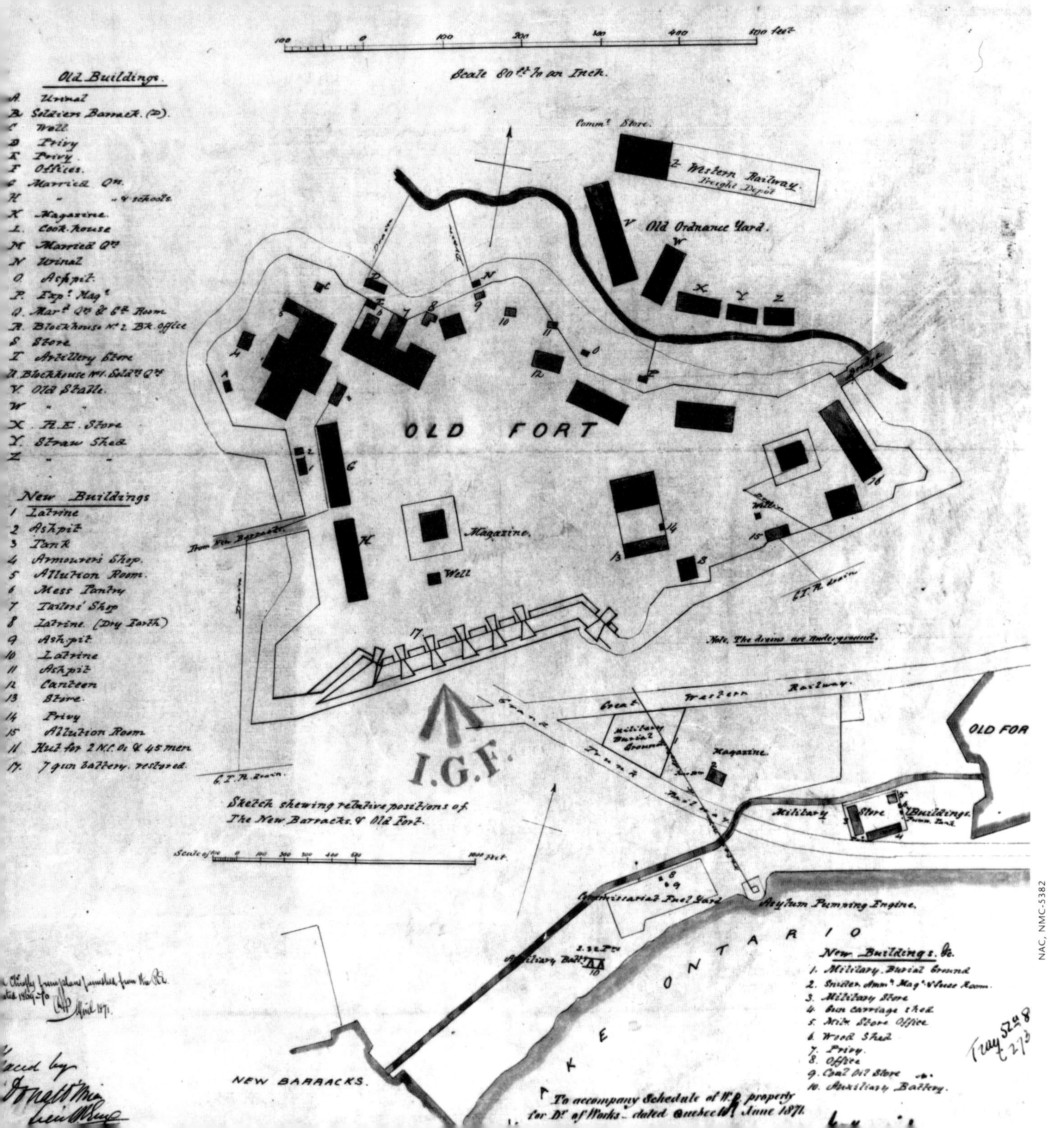

Map 17: This double plan from 1871 shows Fort York on the top; on the bottom, on a much smaller scale, the shoreline between Fort York and the New Fort. On the lower plan, note the magazines and other storehouses, plus the 1860-1911 military cemetery between the Old Fort and New Fort.

fices, storage facilities, and a training ground. In the early 1870s, some of Fort York's buildings served as offices for the military staff of the Toronto Military District, the School of Gunnery (artillery) and School of Military Instruction (infantry), storerooms for the Ontario Rifle Association, and armouries and storerooms for the Toronto Cavalry, Garrison Battery of Artillery, Toronto Field Battery, 2nd Queen's Own Rifles, and the 10th Royal Grenadiers. The government also stored its entire reserve of artillery and small arms ammunition for use by the military west of Toronto at or near the Old Fort.[131]

After 1883, the regular army garrison increased somewhat when "C" Company of the School of Infantry marched into the New Fort. (In the 1890s, the companies of the School of Infantry were organized as the Royal Canadian Regiment.) In 1893, the Royal Canadian Dragoons moved to Toronto, adding a regular army cavalry component to the garrison.[132] In addition to continued use of Fort York as a garrison facility, Canadian troops maintained the fort's harbour defences in the post-Confederation period.[133] This late use of the dilapidated works of Fort York must have been frustrating for the military. In 1871, the Department of Militia and Defence hoped to replace the fort's defences with Martello Towers on the Toronto Island plus a battery at the New Fort as had been recommended by Colonel Jervois in the 1860s. Jervois's extensive landward fortifications were dropped from the plans, perhaps because the army knew that there was no hope of convincing the government to spend the funds that would be required for such a project.[134] In 1888, again resurrecting recommendations made by Jervois over twenty years earlier, the military wanted to maintain heavy artillery on mobile field carriages at Fort York for the defence of Toronto.* Behind this plan was recognition that Fort York was now obsolete since fixed, garrison guns of the type mounted at Fort York "would be of little use at Toronto where there are now no permanent defensive works."[135] Fort York's days as a harbour defence had ended.

The fact that Fort York was maintained so late in the nineteenth century partly overthrows the myth of the "undefended border" between Canada and the United States in the post-War of 1812 period. Even beyond the end of Fort York's defensive capabilities, Canada faced the prospect of war with the United States as late as the Anglo-American clash over the Venezuelan boundary in 1896. There also was some worry over a military threat centred on the Alaska boundary dispute of 1903; in the 1920s, defence planners thought about how to defend the country should the United States invade at the behest of American industrialists wanting to secure access to Canadian raw materials.[136]

After the withdrawal of British regulars, Canada's military resources were adequate to deal with small-scale problems, such as

* The new guns were to be three 25-pounder [11.4 kg] muzzle-loading rifles and either three 20-pounders [9.1 kg] or two 4-inch [10 cm] breach loaders.

putting down the Northwest Rebellion in 1885 and dispatching a military force to the Yukon gold fields in the 1890s to assert Canadian sovereignty. Canada's military capabilities also were sufficient to provide contingents to colonial wars overseas, such as the provision of several thousand men to fight the Boers in the South African War at the turn of the twentieth century. However, if a war broke out with the United States in the late nineteenth or early twentieth centuries, Canada still would have been dependent on large-scale military assistance from Great Britain and the rest of the Empire. Immediately prior to World War I, there were, for example, plans that included counter-attacks by Australian and Indian forces against California should the Americans invade Canada. These were to be launched in co-ordination with British attacks along the Atlantic coast and the defence of Canada itself.[137] Yet, by the turn of the century few people believed that an Anglo-American war was likely; with the entry of the United States into World War I on the side of the British Empire, the odds of war between the two countries seemed to diminish even further.

World War I saw a massive shift in Canadian attitudes towards the military when the country recruited hundreds of thousands of people to fight in Europe. Since large numbers of troops trained in Toronto during World War I, the army took over most of the CNE grounds for "Exhibition Camp" because the existing military facilities were far too small to meet the needs of the army. It was during this period that the New Fort was used for its

MTL, T10220

Pl. 53: One of Toronto's militia regiments, the 48th Highlanders of Canada, in the years between the Boer War and World War I.

MTL, T32419

Pl. 54: Army and Navy veterans deposited their colours at St. John the Evangelist (Garrison) Church on November 19, 1922. When the church closed in the 1950s, the colours and other military relics housed in the building were moved to Canadian Forces Base Borden near Barrie.

most controversial purpose. Enemy aliens – German, Austro-Hungarian, and Turkish citizens – were interred during part of the war. The government processed them through Stanley Barracks before sending them to camps elsewhere in the country. When the war ended, the government used Stanley Barracks to returned these people to Canadian society.[138]

In the 1920s and 1930s, Stanley Barracks and Fort York continued to house the regular army garrison in Toronto. In the 1930s, "Fort York Armoury," built between the old and new forts, opened for the use of some of the city's militia regiments. During World War II, Exhibition Camp re-opened. At the outbreak of war in 1939, Fort York no longer was a military base, having been restored as a historic site museum between 1932 and 1934. However, the war led to the military re-use of parts of Fort York. The army stored ammunition in the Stone Powder Magazine under the protection of the Home Guard, women's groups used the dining room of the Officers' Brick Barracks to package parcels for soldiers overseas, and troops used the grounds as a recreational and drill space.[139] South of the fort, at the Island airport and on the neighbouring mainland, the Royal Norwegian Air Force in exile trained pilots for the war against Hitler.[140] After World War II, the army no longer needed either Fort York or Stanley Barracks. Although Fort York's future as a museum seemed secure at that time, the CNE tore down most of Stanley Barracks, except the officers' barracks, between 1951 and 1953 in an astonishing act of architectural vandalism.

MTL, T11597

Pl. 55: This 1885 view of Fort York shows the South and North Soldiers' Barracks on the left, the 1838 Rebellion Barracks and 1815 Officers' Quarters in the background, and the stockade, which surrounded the 1815 Gunpowder Magazine, on the right.

MTL, T11599

Pl. 56: A late nineteenth-century photograph of the 1815 Officers' Barracks and, in the rear, a cookhouse built in 1838 during the Rebellion Crisis.

THB

Pl. 57: Stanley Barracks at the beginning of the twentieth century. The soldiers carry modern Lee-Enfield Mark I rifles that had been sent from Britain to re-arm Canadian forces during the Venezuelan Crisis.

THB

(Facing page) Pl. 58: Troops drilling at Stanley Barracks during World War I. Pl. 59: The Officers' Mess at Stanley Barracks between the wars.

CHAPTER FOUR

"HISTORIC" FORT YORK

FORT YORK BECOMES A HISTORIC SITE

In the 1880s, at about the same time Fort York's defences became obsolete, people began to see the dilapidated buildings and crumbling walls of the old fort as venerable relics of both the city's earliest history and the War of 1812. Consequently, efforts began to be made to preserve the site, making Fort York one of the earliest places to be considered for historical development in Canada.

In 1889, the City of Toronto wanted the federal government to transfer the fort to its care because of its historical associations. The military responded with a recommendation that the Department of Militia and Defence and the City of Toronto jointly restore the fort grounds for the enjoyment of the public.[1] As was the case so many times with plans developed during the fort's military life, these proposals were not implemented. In the late 1890s, Toronto architect Albert Paul suggested that the fort be restored and that the blockhouses be turned into museums of "the ancient and obsolete arms and accoutrements of which there is an ever increasing store at the fort." Part of Paul's interest was a desire to obtain some work for himself, but part was inspired by his embarrassment at the "disgust of the tourists as they view the dilapidated appearance" of "one of the oldest landmarks of the city."[2] Again, virtually nothing was done at that time.

In 1899, the military authorities agreed to let the Canadian Club erect historical markers at the western entrance to Fort York and at a post-1860 military cemetery located between the old and new forts.*[3] In the first decade of the twentieth century, British army and navy veterans in Toronto erected a memorial to those who fell in the defence of Canada during the War of 1812, located at the original 1793-1860 period graveyard at Victoria Memorial Square northeast of the fort. The designer was Walter Alward Seyward, who later became famous for his Vimy Ridge memorial in France, which commemorates the fallen in Canada's most famous battle of World War I.

Interest in preserving Fort York was part of a broader concern by people in Ontario – particularly those whose families had lived in the province for several generations – to save the physical reminders of the province's early history. The sites of most interest were those connected with the United Empire Loyalists and the War of 1812.[4] These places had the triple advantages of celebrating the British connection, fostering a proud Canadian nationalism within the Empire, and serving as a warning against the perils posed to the Canadian identity by the American republic to the south. In 1909, the lieutenant-governor of Ontario, Sir William Mortimer Clark, gave a speech at Fort York in which he

* The text of one of the marble plaques (erected at a cost of $50) was: "THE OLD FORT, established by Lieut. Governor Simcoe at the mouth of Garrison Creek in 1796 *[sic]* for the Queen's Rangers; occupied by British Troops during the War of 1812-14 and at different times until 1871 *[sic]*. Captured by the Americans April 27, 1813."

MTL, T11619

Pl. 60: When Frank Yeigh took this photograph in 1903, the 1815 South Soldiers' Barracks were married quarters for three military families.

MTL, T13757

Pl. 61: Schoolchildren have visited Fort York on educational field trips since at least the 1890s. Shown here is a class touring the site in 1905 under the supervision of Alexander Muir.

said that the site served a useful purpose in teaching new Canadians that "their country has been fought for, and is worth fighting for again should occasion arise" and that "it is their duty to do their part in upholding and strengthening our Government and institutions" as well as have "impressed on their hearts that we are part of that great British Empire of which we are so justly proud."[5] The chancellor of Victoria College, Nathanael Burwash, declared that if immigrants were to be turned into patriotic Canadians, then "we . . . must make the most of our history and make its monuments as impressive as possible."[6]

The need for preservation was real. As early as the 1850s, developers wanted to demolish the fort and replace it with a lakefront residential project called "Grosvenor Railton." In 1871, the province hoped to acquire Fort York from the federal government to build a prison on the site. In 1890, officials of the Grand Trunk Railway planned to tear down part of the fort's walls to extend their rail lines on the north side of the site. (The GTR already had absorbed military land on the old Garrison Creek site without government permission.) In 1893, the Canadian Pacific Railway sought permission to demolish Fort York and level the hill it sits on so that the space occupied by the fort could be lowered to that of the surrounding rail yards and tracked over, and the soil from the hill could be used as lake fill on the harbour front. In all these cases, military authorities turned down requests to destroy Fort York because the fort continued to fulfil some of

NAC, C-40091

Pl. 62: "Fort York, Toronto, 1890" by Alfred E. Boultbee. From left to right are: Blockhouse No. 2 of 1813, the 1838 cookhouse, the 1814 Blue Barracks, and an 1838 Artillery Barracks.

CTA, DPW, VOL. 5-14

Pl. 63: The west entrance to Fort York at the turn of the twentieth century. Two of Simcoe's condemned cannon, brought to Toronto in the 1790s, can be seen beside the whitewashed barracks, where they were used as bumpers to protect the buildings from wagons and other vehicles.

the army's needs in the Toronto garrison.[7] For its part, the Department of Militia and Defence spent very little money maintaining the fort despite the army's continued use of the site. As a result, the buildings deteriorated badly by the beginning of the twentieth century. It seemed obvious that the historic structures would not survive for many more years without a concerted effort to preserve them.

THE PRESERVATION BATTLE OF 1903-1909

While the Canadian army used Fort York as part of its Toronto base until the 1930s, ownership of the fort and Stanley Barracks passed to the City of Toronto in 1903 when the city purchased the garrison lands for $200,000 after one appraiser declared it to be worth $240,000 and another $300,000.[8] When the city acquired the reserve, it agreed to preserve Fort York and the military cemetery of 1860-1911.[9] The grounds of the 1793-1860 cemetery were not included in this sale, and at this time (1993) are still owned by the Department of National Defence, although the city maintains them as a park.

There was considerable delight by people interested in the historical value of the fort when the city bought the site because they saw the sale as the first step in preserving and developing it as a proper historic site within a larger park setting. However, within two weeks of purchase, the City of Toronto abandoned its preservation commitment and gave the Park-Blackwell Company permission to build a slaughterhouse at the east end of the fort. Park-Blackwell demolished the fort's guardhouse, destroyed the southeast bastion, and cut down the eastern rampart. In the process, workers exposed two graves believed to be those of War of 1812 soldiers. Most of the bones were carted away to a dump along with the rest of the construction debris.[10]

Another danger emerged between 1905 and 1909 that galvanized preservationists and led to a major victory in the war to save Fort York as a historic site. The City of Toronto decided to demolish some of the War of 1812 buildings for a streetcar line to connect the downtown with the Canadian National Exhibition grounds. There still was not enough lake fill south of the fort for a streetcar route at that time, and the city, which owned the CNE, wanted streetcar access to improve attendance at the fair. However, the city was not going to get its way. A teacher from Parkdale Public School, Jean Geeson (who had been bringing her classes to the fort on field trips for years), alerted the heritage community to the danger.[11] The Toronto *Globe* wrote an editorial in favour of saving the fort, and various heritage organizations, led by Barlow Cumberland of the Ontario Historical Society and supported by a large number of influential people, lobbied hard against the city's plans over the next four years.[12] In 1907, Fort York's supporters formed "The Old Fort Protective Association" dedicated to saving the site, with Governor-General Earl Grey as

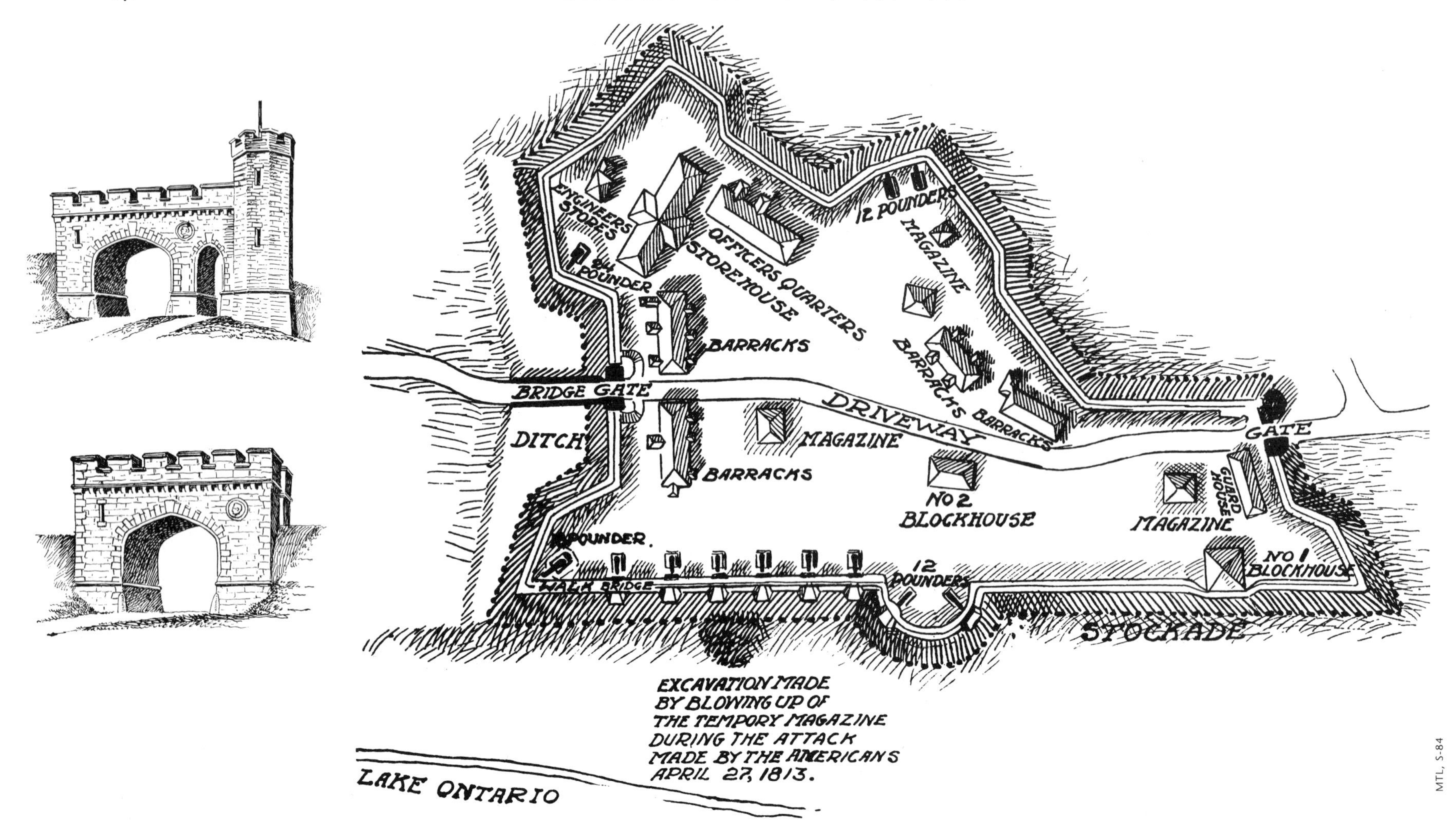

MTL, S-84

Map 18: The Ontario Historical Society prepared this plan in early 1909 showing how the society wanted the fort restored. Key features included the preservation of the extant buildings, the restoration of some of the gun emplacements from the War of 1812 and the Trent Affair, and the installation of the stockade outside of the artillery-proof ramparts. Also planned were mediaeval-looking grand ceremonial gates at each entrance. One (upper left) was to be named after Isaac Brock, the other after John Graves Simcoe, and both were to house public washrooms.

MTL, T11605

Pl. 64: Industrial encroachment consumed the east end of Fort York in the very early years of the twentieth century. Shown here in a 1909 photograph are the East Magazine and Blockhouse Number 1 on the right, with the Park-Blackwell slaughterhouse on the left. The ramp into the slaughterhouse originates to the south of the blockhouse, not in the building as suggested by the photograph.

patron, although it was the Ontario Historical Society that continued to exercise leadership in the battle to save the site.[13] Civic politicians countered these efforts with the feeble argument that a great many people would see whatever parts of the fort survived construction of the line from streetcar windows as they travelled through Fort York on their way to the CNE.

For city council to build the line, money had to be raised through issuing debentures, but before council could take that action, a plebiscite had to be held to approve an enabling by-law. Preservationists fought the by-law, and in 1907 Toronto voters rejected the city's scheme 9,004 to 3,968.[14] City council then rallied to combat the preservationists by using whatever back-room political influence it could command with the provincial and federal governments to defeat its opponents, including a failed attempt to get the provincial legislature to pass an act to allow the city to seek debenture funds without first obtaining the permission of the voters.[15]

By 1908, much of the debate surrounding the streetcar line had evolved into an argument between preservation and commercial growth. The Toronto *Evening News* declared indignantly that the streetcar route would lead to Fort York "being shoved off the map by . . . the commercialism of this later age."[16] In the end, the preservationists won a qualified victory when the City of Toronto agreed not to demolish any of the 1812-period buildings. Yet, during World War I, the north defensive wall and an 1838 cookhouse were destroyed for an alternative streetcar route to the exhibition grounds, and the railways gobbled up whatever fort land they could north of the streetcar line.[17] Today, as a result, the reconstructed north defensive wall largely is located south of its original location.

After World War I, the city changed its attitude and began to preserve the fort grounds by restoring the Trent Affair battery and demolishing the slaughterhouse at the east end of the site. However, the army continued to occupy the fort's historic structures because new facilities "long contemplated by the military authorities" to replace the old fort had not been constructed. The brick soldiers' and officers' barracks and some wood buildings no longer extant served as married quarters until 1933. The blockhouses and East Magazine seem to have been used for storage until about 1932. In 1909, for example, the East Magazine housed three million rounds of ammunition.[18] The Stone Magazine of 1815 served in its original capacity as an ammunition store as late as World War II.[19]

THE 1930s RESTORATION AND THE MUSEUM YEARS

It was a combination of the approaching centennial of the City of Toronto's 1834 incorporation and the need to create jobs for people thrown out of work because of the Great Depression that

MTL, T11604

Pl. 65: This c.1916 photograph shows the streetcar line on the north side of the fort that necessitated the destruction of much of the north curtain wall.

TORONTO HARBOUR COMMISSION ARCHIVES, ARTHUR BEALES COLLECTION, PC 1/1/6284

CTA, SALMON COLL. 609

(Facing page) Pl. 66: The south wall of Fort York in 1922 showing the eroded state of the defences, the embrasures of the Trent Affair Battery, as well as the Stone Magazine and the South Soldiers Barracks.

Pl. 67: The interior of one of the blockhouses at the time of the 1930s restoration.

THB

Pl. 68: Fort York opening-day celebrations on Victoria Day 1934.

(Facing page) Pl. 69: The east end of Fort York in 1934.

CTA, SALMON COLLECTION 810

CTA, SALMON COLLECTION 602

CTA, DPW 52-1541

Pl. 71: This 1932 photograph gives an impression of how the restoration of the walls was a suitable employment project during the Depression because it was so labour intensive. Historically the walls were lined with wood. Inaccurate as the stone is, it now has historical significance as an example of the make-work projects undertaken during the 1930s.

(Facing page) **Pl. 70: The west end of Fort York in 1934, looking south in the days before the Gardiner Expressway destroyed the view towards the lake. In the foreground is the North Soldiers' Barracks of 1815. At that time, only two of its three original rooms survived. The third room was reconstructed about 1960.**

provided the necessary momentum to undertake large-scale preservation and restoration work at Fort York. Most of the work took place between 1932 and 1934 under the leadership of the Ontario Historical Society and the city's mayor, William J. Stewart. The workers on the restoration project were paid out of government job-creation money made available to help alleviate unemployment.[20]

The restorers intended to recreate the garrison as it might have existed in 1816. They chose 1816 as the focus date in part because there existed an excellent map of the fort from that year showing it in its completed state after the War of 1812.[21] In addition to restoring the pre-1816 buildings, the city decided to rebuild missing 1816-period buildings and tear down all later structures. In the end, only one building was dismantled and reconstructed, the Blue Barracks, which incorporated a large quantity of building fabric from the original structure.* All the post-1816 buildings were torn down before the end of 1934. Restoration practices were in their infancy in Canada at that time and mistakes were made. The loss of the post-1816 buildings

* Half of the 1814 original Blue Barracks was torn down at the time of the Rebellion Crisis to create a better field of fire for troops in Blockhouse Number 2 in case rebels over-ran the fort. The remainder of the building was dismantled in the 1930s except for its four chimneys. The restorers poured a cement pad to serve as a foundation and floor, then rebuilt the barracks, using as much original wood as possible.

MTL, 2238

Pl. 72: One of the exhibits installed in 1934, showing the lifestyles of officers as understood at that time.

was tragic, as structures such as the large Rebellion Barracks in the northwest bastion held legitimacy as part of the country's turbulent military history. The architects and workers restored the War of 1812 buildings clumsily. They removed the early clapboard from the 1813 blockhouses to expose the squared timber construction underneath in the mistaken assumption that clapboard was not historically appropriate for the 1816-period. Yet the fact that the fort survived at all is a cause for considerable thankfulness, especially in contrast to the sad loss of Stanley Barracks twenty years later.

On Victoria Day 1934, the governor-general, the Earl of Bessborough, officially opened "Old Fort York" as a historic site museum. On hand were representatives of the Toronto military, many dressed in reproductions of historical uniforms to depict the units that served at Fort York in its early days, such as the Queen's Rangers of 1793 and the York Militia of 1812. Other celebrants included Ukrainian dancers who represented the nascent multicultural quality of Toronto's character. It was a beautiful day and the crowd in attendance was enormous, far exceeding predictions.[22] Some of the buildings housed period-room exhibits, such as the blockhouses, which contained bunks to represent their original use as barracks. In other buildings, voluntary historical associations, such as the United Empire Loyalists and the Women's Canadian Historical Society, presented more traditional "glass case" museum exhibits. Once the museum was opened, the City of Toronto Parks Department managed Fort York in the 1930s and 1940s.

By the end of World War II, the fort had become dilapidated again and had to be re-restored. The city created the Toronto Civic Historical Committee to carry out the necessary work and transferred the fort from the jurisdiction of the Parks Department to the committee. This committee became the Toronto Historical Board in 1960. The THB continues to be the city agency responsible for maintaining and operating Fort York along with other city-owned museums. After some re-restoration work in the early 1950s, Fort York re-opened as a historic site on June 14, 1953. On September 30, it closed for the winter. Throughout the 1950s, the committee undertook more restoration work and expanded visitor services. The committee gradually replaced the older exhibits installed by the different historical societies with its own – a process that THB staff continued into the 1960s. Fort staff gave guided tours to the public from 1953, and 1955 saw the formation of the "Fort York Guard" to help recreate some of the sights and sounds of an early nineteenth century garrison by performing drills and other demonstrations. In 1957, female staff, costumed to represent some of the women associated with the fort's history, joined the all-male guard.[23]

THE GARDINER EXPRESSWAY THREAT

A new danger to the survival of Fort York and the garrison cemetery of 1860-1911 arose in the late 1950s when the Metropolitan Toronto government wanted to build the new Gardiner Expressway through the site.*

In January 1958, Metro planners declared their intention to tear down the fort and rebuild it close to the waterfront. To support the demolition of the fort, Metro politicians and civil servants argued that the fort's authentic environment had been lost by lake fill operations between the 1850s and the 1920s. Therefore, rebuilding the fort at a new location close to the waterfront would create a sense of the fort's original geographic context. Given the reconstruction standards of the 1950s, there can be no doubt that the authentic War of 1812 buildings would have been lost, and that a new Fort York, at best, would have contained pathetic copies of the original structures. Furthermore, the fort's archaeological resource would have been sub-

* The Metropolitan Toronto government should not be confused with the City of Toronto government. Metro was created in 1953 when a number of Toronto area municipalities gave up some of their powers (such as police and some road responsibilities) to create an efficient higher level of government while other responsibilities (such as fire protection) were retained by the local governments. The relationship is somewhat analogous to that of several rural township governments within a larger county government.

TORONTO STAR

Pl. 73: A 1959 *Toronto Star* editorial cartoon by Duncan Macpherson celebrates the defeat of Metro politicians in the Gardiner Expressway battle.

stantially destroyed, and the birthplace of the city and an important battlefield site would have been forgotten under a jumble of elevated roadways.

The Toronto Civic Historical Committee, with the support of the province's historical societies, did its best to counter Metro's arguments. Despite these efforts, the committee seemed to be fighting a losing battle as the city, Metro, and the provincial government, as well as the media, all supported moving the fort.[24] In January 1959, the anti-Fort York offensive began to falter when the *Toronto Star* changed its position and advocated the preservation of the fort *in situ*.[25] Subsequently, Metro reversed itself and allowed the fort to remain on its original site. Metro built the Gardiner Expressway south of the fort, seriously degrading the fort's atmosphere, but at least preserving the important heritage resources of the site. Ultimately, a combination of factors saved Fort York. One was the massive cost of rebuilding the fort compared to moving the expressway a little further south than initially planned. Other factors were a combination of the original agreement between the city and the federal government guaranteeing the preservation of the site and the public support the preservationists had mustered in their battle with Metro.[26]

After winning the expressway battle, THB staff continued to develop new exhibits, restore the heritage buildings, and expand visitor services. To meet growing demands by the public

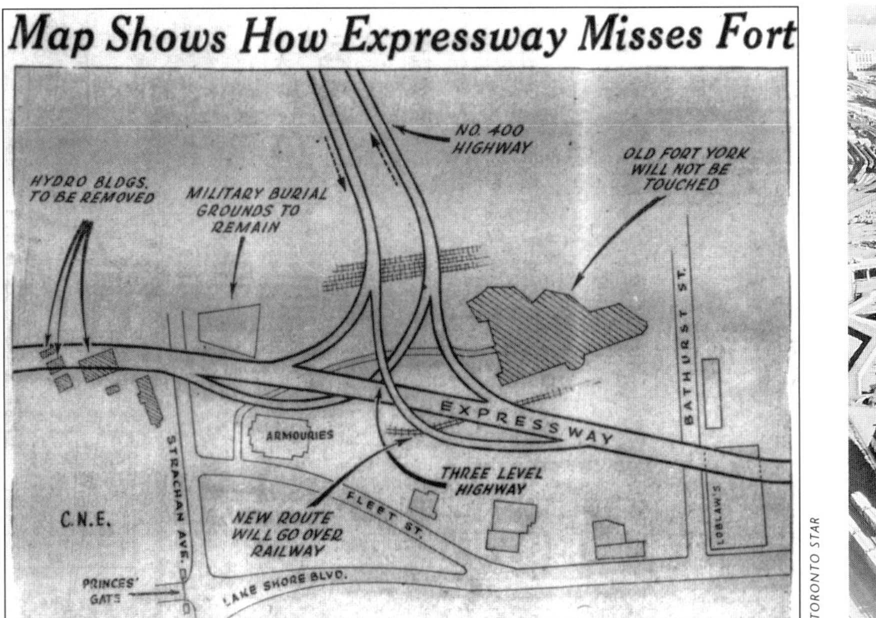

TORONTO STAR

Map 19: The *Toronto Star* printed this map in 1959 showing how the fort was to be saved by re-routing the Gardiner Expressway to the south. Fortunately, the links with Highway 400 were never constructed.

RECORDS AND ARCHIVES DIVISION, METROPOLITAN TORONTO

Pl. 74: The Gardiner Expressway under construction near Fort York in 1960.

and the educational community, staff developed new programmes and opened the site on a year-round basis. As with most historic site museums, site restoration and exhibit development continue to be ongoing activities to address changing visitor interests, new preservation technologies, advancements in historical research, and to counteract the inevitable deterioration caused by the climate, pollution, visitor traffic, and a host of other unavoidable problems. A constant problem over the years has been the limited amount of financial resources made available to carry out this work. As a result, the THB has had to struggle constantly to maintain the site properly and keep up with changes in public expectations and museological standards.

THE FORT YORK HERITAGE CONSERVATION DISTRICT

In 1985, the City of Toronto designated Fort York, Garrison Common, and a part of the old garrison reserve at the corner of Fleet Street and Strachan Avenue as the "Fort York Heritage Conservation District" under the Ontario Heritage Act. This designation was symbolic of a new level of recognition by the city and its residents of Fort York's critical historical significance. Beyond symbolism, designation provided legal recognition of the importance of the district and improved the city's ability to preserve the district's historical resources. Yet vigilance continues to be necessary. As late as 1986 consultants employed by the Metropolitan Toronto government seriously studied putting roadways through and over the conservation district.[27] Fortunately, revised plans more sympathetic to the needs of the district were developed for implementation instead of those initially proposed. Another step to secure the fort's future occurred in 1987 when the Historic Sites and Monuments Board of Canada declared the buildings at Fort York to be of national significance in the country's history.

Today, in addition to being one of the country's major military museums, Fort York is a critically important heritage resource linking us tangibly to so many dramatic parts of our history, particularly to the formative days of Upper Canada's first settlement in the late eighteenth and early nineteenth centuries when American desires to annex British North America were strongest. The survival and preservation of Fort York places Toronto in an enviable position because very few large cities possess such a direct and important physical connection to their very beginnings. The challenge for the future is to develop and manage this resource at the highest museological standards possible so that it is preserved and interpreted for the education and enjoyment of everyone interested in our history.

MTL, T2237

Pl. 75: The mess exhibit in the Officers' Brick Barracks as it appeared in the 1960s. This exhibit was upgraded substantially in 1968 and replaced altogether with a new interpretation of the Officers' Mess in 1993.

THB

Pl. 76: The Toronto Historical Board undertook archaeological work beginning in the 1980s in connection with ongoing restoration work. In this photograph, data are being collected on the south side of Blockhouse No. 2 in 1992. Archaeological discoveries have proved to be critically important in informing curatorial staff on how to restore architectural features and re-interpret the life of the garrison community.

(Facing page) Pl. 77: An aerial view of Fort York today, showing how much the environment has changed since the Queen's Rangers began to clear the bush to build the fort on the shore of Lake Ontario in 1793. Note the location of the old shoreline, shown by the dotted line.

THB

ONTARIO MINISTRY OF NATURAL RESOURCES

ENDNOTES

Whenever original documents have been published, they have been listed in the endnotes according to their published form rather than to the archives in which they are housed to make research easier for anyone who wants to pursue the information in this book further. Dates are given in metric style: year/month/day, hence, October 2, 1793 is 1793.10.02.

A NOTE ABOUT THE NAME "FORT YORK"

1. Peter Russell to Aeneas Shaw, 1797.07.18, Edith G. Firth, ed., *The Town of York, 1793-1815* (Toronto, 1962), p. 63.
2. *Canadian Illustrated News*, 1876.04.15, vol. 12, p. 251.

CHAPTER ONE

1. Instructions to Gother Mann, 1788.05.29, NAC, Record Group 8, British Military Records (hereafter RG8), C Series, vol. 381.
2. For a more complete discussion of the military situation leading to the founding of Toronto, see: Carl Benn, "The Military Context of the Founding of Toronto," *Ontario History*, vol. 81, 1989, pp. 303-322. Broader discussion of the frontier crisis of the 1780s and 1790s, can be read in: A. L. Burt, *The United States, Great Britain, and British North America from the Revolution to the Establishment of Peace after the War of 1812* (New Haven, 1940), pp. 16-184; Wiley Sword, *President Washington's Indian War: The Struggle for the Old Northwest, 1790-1795* (Norman, Okla., 1985); and, J. Mackay Hitsman, *Safeguarding Canada: 1763-1870* (Toronto, 1968), pp. 46-65.
3. Bil Gilbert, *God Gave Us This Country: Tekamthi and the First American Civil War* (New York, 1989), pp. 158, 169.

4. Thomas Jefferson to James Monroe, 1793.05.05, E. A. Cruikshank, ed., *The Correspondence of Lieut. Governor John Graves Simcoe*, hereafter SP (Toronto, 1923-1931), vol. 1, p. 328.
5. John Graves Simcoe to Sir Alured Clarke, 1793.05.31, SP, vol. 1, pp. 339-343.
6. *Ibid.*, pp. 338-343.
7. Jacob Spelt, *Urban Development in South-Central Ontario* (Toronto, 1972), p. 26.
8. J. M. S. Careless, *Toronto to 1918* (Toronto, 1984), p. 11.
9. Simcoe to Clarke, 1793.05.31, SP, vol. 1, p. 343.
10. Elizabeth Simcoe, 1793.07.20, *The Diary of Mrs. John Graves Simcoe*, John Ross Robertson, ed. (Toronto, 1911), p. 176.
11. Elizabeth Simcoe Diary, 1793.07.29&30, p. 179; and *Upper Canada Gazette*, 1793.08.01.
12. J. G. Simcoe to Clarke, 1793.05.31, SP, vol. 1, p. 343.
13. J. G. Simcoe to Clarke, 1793.05.31; same to same, 1793.06.04; Robert Pilkington to J. G. Simcoe, 1793.09.06; and J. G. Simcoe to the Duke of Richmond, 1793.09.23, SP, vol. 1, pp. 339-340, 347, and vol. 2, pp. 47-48, 67.
14. Minutes of the Executive Council, 1793.09.23, Edith G. Firth, ed., *The Town of York, 1793-1815* (Toronto, 1962), pp. 11-14.
15. General Order, 1793.08.26; J. G. Simcoe to Henry Dundas, 1792.11.04, SP vol. 2, p. 46, and vol. 1, p. 246; and William Renwick Riddell, *The Life of John Graves Simcoe* (Toronto, 1926), p. 229, n. 14.
16. J. G. Simcoe to Dundas, 1793.06.17, SP, vol. 1, p. 357.
17. Clarke to J. G. Simcoe, 1793.06.14, SP, vol. 1, p. 355.
18. Careless, p. 21; and Baron Dorchester to J. G. Simcoe, 1794.01.27, SP, vol. 2, pp. 136-137.
19. John Andre, *Infant Toronto as Simcoe's Folly* (Toronto, 1967), p. 37.
20. J. G. Simcoe to Dundas, 1793.09.20; and J. G. Simcoe to Dorchester, 1794.09.05, SP, vol. 2, p. 57, and vol. 3, p. 42.
21. Clarke to J. G. Simcoe, 1793.06.14; and, J. G. Simcoe to Dundas, 1793.09.20, SP, vol. 1, p. 355, and vol. 2, p. 63.
22. David Shank and Robert Pilkington Memorandum, 1793.09.01, NAC, RG8, C, vol. 546; J. G. Simcoe to Richmond, 1793.09.23 and 1793.11.22, SP, vol. 2, pp. 68, 108; and Carl Benn, *The King's Mill on the Humber, 1793-1803* (Etobicoke, 1979), p. 2.
23. J. G. Simcoe to Dundas, 1793.10.19, SP, vol. 2, pp. 90-91.
24. J. G. Simcoe to Dorchester, 1794.10.24, SP, vol. 3, p. 149; and General Statement of Public Property, *c.*1800, Firth, pp. 51-52.
25. A Plan of Blockhouses, 1794.08.20, MTL.
26. Elizabeth Simcoe Diary, 1793.08.24, p. 187.
27. J. G. Simcoe to the Committee of the Privy Council for Trade and Plantations, 1794.12.20, SP, vol. 3, p. 192. See also: Ronald J. Stagg, "Berczy, William," *Dictionary of Canadian Biography*, vol. 5, 1801-1820. (Toronto, 1976); and F. R. Berchem, *The Yonge Street Story, 1763-1860* (Toronto, 1977), pp. 7-37.
28. William Jarvis to Samuel Peters, 1794.03.28, A. H. Young, ed., "Letters from the Secretary of Upper Canada and Mrs. Jarvis, to her Father, the Rev. Samuel Peters D.D.," *Annual Report and Transaction No. 23 of the Women's Canadian Historical Society of Toronto, 1922-1923* (Toronto, 1923), p. 34.
29. J. G. Simcoe Memorandum, 1794.03.24, SP, vol. 2, pp. 192-193.
30. Dorchester to J. G. Simcoe, 1794.04.14, SP, vol. 2, p. 202.
31. Sword, p. 306.
32. Peter Russell to Robert Prescott, 1796.09.29, E. A. Cruikshank, ed., *The Correspondence of the Honourable Peter Russell*, hereafter RP (Toronto, 1932-1936), vol. 1, p. 51.

33. Berchem, p. 35.
34. Benn, *King's Mill, passim.*
35. Unfortunately, the chief's wife's name is not known.
36. Leo A. Johnson, "The Mississauga-Lake Ontario Land Surrender of 1805," *Ontario History*, vol. 83, *passim.*
37. Donald B. Smith, *Sacred Feathers: The Reverend Peter Jones (Kahkewaquonaby) & the Mississauga Indians* (Toronto, 1987), pp. 27-31.
38. *Ibid.*, p. 28; Russell to J. G. Simcoe, 1796.12.31, RP, vol. 1, p. 117; and The King *vs.* Charles McCuen, 1796.00.00, Firth, pp. 84-85.
39. Smith, p. 28.
40. Russell to Aeneas Shaw, 1797.07.18, Firth, p. 63.
41. Russell to the Duke of Portland, 1798.03.21, RP, vol. 2, pp. 122-123; and Isaac Weld, *Travels through the States of North America and the Provinces of Upper and Lower Canada during the Years 1795, 1796, and 1797*, 4th ed. (London, 1807), vol. 2, pp. 84-85.
42. Prescott to Russell, 1797.06.21, Firth, pp. 62-63.
43. *Ibid.*
44. John McGill to J. G. Simcoe, 1798.02.24, RP, vol. 2, p. 102.
45. Russell to Portland, 1797.08.19 and 1798.01.21, Firth, pp. 64-65.
46. Russell to Prescott, 1798.01.21, Firth, pp. 64-65.
47. Russell to Prescott, 1797.08.19, Firth, p. 64; and Russell to J. G. Simcoe, 1797.12.09, RP, vol. 2, p. 38.
48. General Statement of Public Property, *c.*1800, Firth, p. 53.
49. Smith, pp. 28-29.
50. David Shank to James Green, 1798.10.10, NAC, RG8, C, vol. 512.
51. J. G. Simcoe to Richmond, 1793.11.23, SP, vol. 2, p. 108.
52. Report of the State of Public Works and Buildings, 1802.09.12, Firth, pp. 71-72.
53. Watercolour of the York garrison by Sempronius Stretton, "York Barracks, Lake Ontario, Upper Canada, Anno Domini 1804," NAC, C-14905.
54. Floor plan of Government House, 1800, NAC, NMC-5428.
55. J. G. Simcoe to Dorchester, 1796.03.02, SP, vol. 4, p. 206.

CHAPTER TWO

1. Marshall Smelser, *The Democratic Republic: 1801-1815* (New York, 1968), p. 285.
2. Richard Glover, *Britain at Bay: Defence Against Bonaparte, 1803-1814* (London, 1973), pp. 68-72.
3. For complete discussions of the causes of the War of 1812, see: J. C. A. Stagg, *Mr. Madison's War: Politics, Diplomacy, and Warfare in the Early American Republic, 1783-1830* (Princeton, 1983), pp. 3-119; Roger R. Brown, *The Republic in Peril* (New York, 1964); Bradford Perkins, *The Causes of the War of 1812: National Honor or National Interest?* (New York, 1962); and, George F. G. Stanley, *The War of 1812: Land Operations* (Ottawa, 1983), pp. 3-43.
4. Ralph Bruyères Report Relative to the Present State of York Upper Canada, 1812.04.22, Edith G. Firth, ed., *The Town of York, 1793-1815* (Toronto, 1962), p. 78.
5. Isaac Brock to Sir George Prevost, 1812.04.22, NAC, Record Group 8, hereafter RG8, C Series, British Military Records, vol. 676; Bruyères, Report Relative to the Present State of York, Upper Canada, *c.*1812.03.00, Firth, pp. 77-78; and Ned Myers, *Ned Myers; or, a Life Before the Mast*, James Fenimore Cooper, ed., 1843 (reprinted: Annapolis, 1989), p. 64.

6. A. H. Pye to Prevost, 1811.12.07, William S. Dudley, ed., *The Naval War of 1812* (Washington, 1985), pp. 268-273.
7. Andrew Gray Report Upon the Expediency of Removing the Marine Establishment from Kingston to York, 1812.03.12, Firth, pp. 78-80.
8. *Ibid.*, p. 80.
9. Noah Freer to Brock, 1812.04.27, Firth, p. 80.
10. *Ibid.*, p. 81.
11. C. Winton-Clare, "A Shipbuilder's War," Morris Zaslow, ed., *The Defended Border* (Toronto, 1964), pp. 167, 169.
12. Thomas Jefferson to William Duane, 1812.08.04, Stagg, p. 5, n. 8.
13. E. A. Cruikshank, "Record of the Services of Canadian Regiments in the War of 1812: Part XIII. – The York Militia," Canadian Military Institute *Selected Papers*, no. 16, 1908, p. 39; and "Papers Loaned by T. R. Kennedy, Levis, Que., of Capt. H. Pringle," Women's Canadian Historical Society of Toronto *Transactions*, no. 5, 1905.
14. Cruikshank, p. 38; and William Chewett, Regimental Order, 1812.09.12, E. A. Cruikshank, ed., *The Documentary History of the Campaigns upon the Niagara Frontier in 1812-14*, hereafter DH (Niagara Falls and Welland, 1902-1908), vol. 3, p. 240.
15. General Order, 1812.10.19, NAC, RG8, C, vol. 1203; and Memorandum re Isaac Benn escorting American prisoners from York to Kingston in April 1813, 1816.07.10, AO, Heir and Devisee Commission, Ms. 657, R. 17, Parcel 5: 1813-1816.
16. George Sheppard, "'Deeds Speak': Militiamen, Medals, and the Invented Traditions of 1812," *Ontario History*, vol. 83, 1990, *passim.*
17. Firth, p. lxxxvii; and *Report of the Loyal and Patriotic Society of Upper Canada* (Montreal, 1817), *passim.*
18. Comparative Statement of the British and American Forces upon the Lakes, 1813.03.13, DH, vol. 5, p. 111.
19. John Armstrong to Henry Dearborn, 1813.02.10, DH, vol. 5, pp. 66-67.
20. Dearborn-Armstrong Correspondence, various dates, DH, vol. 5, pp. 70-73, 78, 87, 102-103.
21. Dearborn to Armstrong, n.d., DH, vol. 5, p. 142.
22. Stagg, pp. 284-288; 335-336; 335, n. 118.
23. *Ibid.*, pp. 286-288, 335, n. 118.
24. Bruyères to Provost, 1813.01.28, Firth, pp. 288-289.
25. *Ibid.*, p. 289.
26. Gilbert Auchinleck, *A History of the War between Great Britain and the United States of America during the Years 1812, 1813, and 1814*, 1855 (reprinted: London, 1972), p. 155.
27. *Ibid.*
28. DH, vol. 5, p. 161; Cromwell Pearce Account, n.d. (Firth, pp. 303-306); Broadside: *Victory by General Dearborn*, 1813.05.01, Carl Benn, *The Battle of York* (Belleville, Ont., 1984), p. 42; *The United States Gazette*, 1813.05.13, DH, vol. 5, p. 160; Joseph Thatcher to Carl Benn, 1990.03.13, Fort York Correspondence Files; Theodore Roosevelt, *Naval War of 1812*, 1882 (reprinted: Annapolis, 1987), p. 214; and George F. Emmons, comp., *The Navy of the United States from the Commencement, 1775 to 1853* (Washington, 1853).

Data on the size and composition of the American forces is confusing. The number of soldiers is based on Dearborn's letter to Armstrong written before setting sail on April 23, 1813; in it he stated he had 1,600 men and expected another 150 to join him shortly. With the delay in leaving Sackett's Harbor, there seems to have been no reason for the 150 extra men to have not joined the force. Cromwell Pearce's account of the battle lists the infantry regiments that participated. In his record, Pearce states that the 6th, 15th, and

16th Regiments were present along with one company of the 14th and a "detachment" of the 21st. The company of riflemen is assumed to have come from the 1st Regiment because the riflemen's commander at York was Major Benjamin Forsyth from that corps. The geographic origins of the volunteers are described in a broadside issued immediately after the battle. The 3rd Artillery is identified in an article published in *The United States Gazette* on May 13, 1813, although there are other contemporary references that indicate that the Light Artillery also were present, as one of their officers was in the battle. The presence of marines is assumed because of the naval component of the force and because Marines' material dating from the war has been recovered archaeologically at Sackett's Harbor. The composition of the naval squadron was:

VESSEL	ARMAMENT
Madison (ship)	24 short 32-pounders
Oneida (brig)	16 short 24-pounders
Hamilton (schooner)	1 long 32-pounder
	1 long 24-pounder
	8 long 6-pounders
Scourge (schooner)	1 long 32-pounder
	8 short 12-pounders
Conquest (schooner)	1 long 12-pounder
	4 long 6-pounders
Tompkins (schooner)	1 long 12-pounder
	6 long 6-pounders
Julia (schooner)	1 long 32-pounder
	1 long 12-pounder
Growler (schooner)	1 long 32-pounder
	1 long 12-pounder
Ontario (schooner)	1 long 32-pounder
	1 long 12-pounder
Fair American (schooner)	1 long 24-pounder
	1 long 12-pounder
Pert (schooner)	1 long 24-pounder
Asp (schooner)	1 long 24-pounder
Lady of the Lake (schooner)	1 long 9-pounder
Raven (transport)	1 ?.

29. William Dummer Powell Account, n.d.; Powell Narrative, n.d.; and William Allan Ms., 1813.05.08, DH, vol. 5, pp. 175, 203, 192-193.

30. Return of Garrison Ordnance; and Return of Field Ordnance & Travelling Carriages, 1813.03.31, NAC, RG8, C, vol. 387; E. A. Cruikshank, "The Garrisons of Toronto and York, 1750-1850," Canadian Military Institute *Selected Papers*, no. 31, 1934-1935, pp. 57-58; Powell Account, n.d., DH, vol. 5, p. 175; and Myers, p. 64.

There are two conflicting documents describing the guns at York. The first lists two 18-pounders, two 12-pounders, six 6-pounders, and eight 18-pounder carronades. The second lists two light 6-pounder brass guns. This totals twenty guns. However the carronades seem not to have been mounted, but were located at the dockyard with the *Sir Isaac Brock*, probably ready to be placed on her decks at the earliest possible moment to sail from York. Given the short range of the carronades, it is debatable whether they would have been useful in the crucial early stages of the battle when the tide could have been turned by driving away the American squadron, although they may have been useful against the American army once it landed. The 12-pounders mounted on field carriages before the war seem to have been moved away from York sometime before the battle or had become unserviceable. This leaves twelve guns to be accounted for. William Dummer Powell, writing just after the battle, placed two 6-pounders at the garrison (east of modern Bathurst Street), two 12-pounders at the Government House Battery (today's Circular Battery), and two 18-pounders at the Western Battery. He obviously forgot the French 18-pounder in the creek valley mentioned in Ned Myers's account of the battle. Where the other six 6-pounders were is not known. The two light 6-pounders guns seem to have been mounted on field carriages for mobile deployment although they do not seem to have been used in the battle; the others possibly were at Gibraltar Point and at the Town Blockhouse.

31. P. Finan, *Journal of a Voyage to Quebec in the Year 1825, with Recollections of Canada during the late American War in the Years 1812-13* (London, 1828), DH, vol. 5., p. 207; Sir Roger Sheaffe to Edward Baynes, 1813.04.10, Sheaffe Letterbook, *Publications of the Buffalo Historical Society*, vol. 17, 1913, p. 373; Sheaffe to Prevost, 1813.05.05; Allan Ms., 1813.05.08; Bruyères to Prevost, 1813.02.13; Sir James Lucas Yeo to John Wilson Croker, 1813.05.26, DH, vol. 5, pp. 190, 201, 217-219, 244; Terms of Capitulation of York, 1813.04.27, Firth, pp. 296-298; Nominal List of the Killed, Wounded[,] Prisoners, & Missing of the Troops engaged at York, 1813.05.10, Jesse Edgar Middleton, *The Municipality of Toronto: A History* (Toronto, 1923), pp. 120-121; Cruikshank, "Garrisons of Toronto," p. 58; and NAC, Record Group 9, Militia Papers, 187, Pay List, 1813.04.24.
32. Sheaffe to Prevost, 1813.05.05; and Powell Account, DH, vol. 5, pp. 189, 176.
33. Allan Ms., 1813.05.08; and Sheaffe to Prevost, 1813.05.05, DH, vol. 5, pp. 193, 189.
34. Sheaffe to Prevost, 1813.05.05, DH, vol. 5, p. 189.
35. ______ Fraser to the Philadelphia *Aurora*, 1813.05.00; Powell Account, n.d.; and Sheaffe to Prevost, 1813.05.05, DH, vol. 5, pp. 179-181, 176, 189.
36. Officer of the United States Army to the *United States Gazette*, 1813.05.09; Allen Ms., 1813.05.08; Fraser to the Philadelphia *Aurora*, 1813.05.00; Finan, DH, vol. 5, pp. 214, 193, 180-181, 208; Pearce Account, n.d.; and John Beikie to Miles Macdonell, 1814.03.19, Firth, pp. 304, 329.
37. Fraser to the Philadelphia *Aurora*, 1813.05.00; Powell Narrative, n.d.; and Dearborn to Daniel Tompkins, 1813.04.28, DH, vol. 5, pp. 180, 206, 170; and Pearce Account, n.d., Firth, p. 304.
38. Fraser to the Philadelphia *Aurora*, 1813.05.00; Dearborn to Armstrong, 1813.04.28; and Powell Account, n.d., DH, vol. 5, pp. 180, 167, 176.
39. Allan Ms., 1813.05.08, DH, vol. 5, p. 192.
40. Fraser to the Philadelphia *Aurora*, 1813.05.00; Isaac Chauncey to the Sec. of the Navy, 1813.04.28; and Sheaffe to Prevost, 1813.05.05, DH, vol. 5, pp. 181, 169, 190; and Myers, p. 60.
41. Sheaffe to Prevost, 1813.05.05; Finan; and Fraser to the Philadelphia *Aurora*, 1813.05.00, DH, vol. 5, pp. 190, 209, 181; and Pearce Account, n.d., Firth, p. 304.
42. W. E. Hollon, "Zebulon Montgomery Pike and the York Campaign, 1813," *New York History*, vol. 30, 1949, p. 267.
43. Ely Playter Diary, 1813.04.27, Firth, p. 280; and Sheaffe to Prevost, 1813.05.05, DH, vol. 5, p. 190.
44. Dearborn to Armstrong, 1813.04.28; Fraser to the Philadelphia *Aurora*, 1813.05.00; and Allan Ms., 1813.05.08, DH, vol. 5, pp. 167, 182, 203; and Myers, pp. 61, 64.
45. Myers, pp. 64-65.

46. Sheaffe to Prevost, 1813.05.05, DH, vol. 5, p. 190.
47. List of losses suffered by different officers in the Battle of York, including Q.M. Finan of the Royal Nfld. Regt., n.d., *c.*1813, NAC, RG8, C, vol. 84.
48. Finan, DH, vol. 5, p. 209.
49. Samuel S. Conner to Armstrong, 1813.05.04, Donald R. Hickey, *The War of 1812* (Chicago, 1989), p. 129.
50. *Niles Weekly Register*, 1813.06.12, DH, vol. 5, p. 182.
51. George Howard to Sarah Howard, 1813.05.07, Hickey, p. 129.
52. Hollon, p. 271.
53. Pearce Account, n.d., Firth, p. 305; and Fraser to the Philadelphia *Aurora*, 1813.05.00, DH, vol. 5, p. 182.
54. Pearce Account, n.d., Firth, p. 305.
55. Myers, p. 61.
56. Sheaffe to Prevost, 1813.05.05, DH, vol. 5, p. 191.
57. Finan, DH, vol. 5, p. 210; and Robert Barclay to Freer, 1813.05.09, William C. H. Wood, ed., *Select British Documents of the Canadian War of 1812* (Toronto, 1920-1928), vol. 1, pp. 115-119.
58. Playter Diary, 1813.04.27, Firth, p. 280.
59. Pearce Account, n.d., Firth, p. 305.
60. Allan Ms., 1813.05.08, DH, vol. 5, p. 196; and John Strachan to James Brown, 1813.04.26/1813.06.14, Firth, pp. 294-295.
61. Total Killed, Wounded, Prisoners & Missing at York, 1813.04.27, Firth, p. 310 and n. 53; and *Niles Weekly Register*, 1813.06.12, DH, vol. 5, p. 183.
62. Strachan to Brown, 1813.04.26/1813.06.14, Firth, p. 295.
63. Terms of Capitulation, 1813.04.27, Firth, pp. 296-298.
64. Allan Ms., 1813.05.08, DH, vol. 5, p. 196.
65. Isaac Wilson to Jonathan Wilson, 1813.12.05, Firth, p. 293.
66. Playter Diary, 1813.04.29, Firth, p. 281; and Description of the Attack and Occupation of York, 1813.*c.*05.00, Women's Canadian Historical Society of Toronto *Transactions*, no. 5, 1905, p. 4.
67. John Beikie Memorandum, *c.*1813.05.00, Firth, p. 300.
68. Angelique Givins Losses, n.d.; and Supplementary Statement, 1815.10.03, Firth, pp. 301-302.
69. Penelope Beikie to John MacDonnell, 1813.05.05, Firth, p. 300.
70. Strachan to Brown, 1813.04.26/1813.06.14, Firth, p. 296; Letter to the *Kingston Gazette*, 1813.08.17, Charles. W. Humphries, "The Capture of York," Zaslow, p. 263.
71. Charles P. Stacey, *The Battle of Little York* (Toronto, 1971), pp. 18-20; and Humphries, pp. 262-264.
72. William Beaumont Diary, 1813.05.01 and 1813.05.11, Jesse S. Myer, *Life and Letters of Dr. William Beaumont* (St. Louis, 1939), pp. 45-46.
73. Deposition of Duncan Cameron Concerning Benjamin Thrall, 1813.08.16, Firth, pp. 309-310.
74. Strachan to Brown, 1813.04.26/1813.06.14, Firth, p. 296.
75. W. W. Baldwin to Quetton St. George, 1814.07.20, Firth, p. 332.
76. Meeting of the Magistrates, 1813.04.30, Firth, p. 299.
77. Description of the Attack and Occupation of York, 1813.*c.*05.00, Women's Canadian Historical Society of Toronto *Transactions*, no. 5, 1905, p. 4.
78. Strachan to Brown, 1813.04.26/1813.06.14; and Mrs. W. D. Powell to Powell, 1813.05.10, Firth, pp. 295-296, 310-311.
79. Beaumont Diary, 1813.04.27, p. 44.
80. Pearce Account, n.d., Firth, p. 305.
81. Benn, pp. 45-51.
82. *Quebec Mercury*, 1813.05.25, DH, vol. 5, p. 211.
83. Strachan to Brown, 1813.04.26/1813.06.14, Firth, p. 296.

84. John Beikie to Macdonell, 1814.03.19, Firth, p. 329.
85. J. Mackay Hitsman, *The Incredible War of 1812* (Toronto, 1972), p. 127.
86. John Norton, *The Journal of Major John Norton*, 1816, Carl F. Klinck and James T. Talman, eds. (Toronto, 1970), pp. 318-320.
87. Mrs. Powell to Powell, 1813.05.12, Firth, p. 311.
88. Stagg, p. 335, n. 118.
89. Dearborn to Armstrong, pre-1813.04.27, DH, vol. 5, p. 142.
90. Sheaffe to the Earl of Bathurst, 1813.04.05, DH, vol. 6, p. 147.
91. Dearborn to Armstrong, 1813.04.28, DH, vol. 5, p. 168.
92. Firth, p. 308, n. 1.
93. Sheaffe to Bathurst, 1813.05.13, Firth, pp. 311-312; and Humphries, pp. 261-262.
94. Stacey, p. 21.
95. Jacob Brown to Tompkins, 1813.06.01, DH, vol. 5, p. 286; and Myers, p. 65.
96. Powell Account and Narrative, n.d.; and Allan Ms., 1813.05.08, DH, vol. 5, pp. 175, 203, 192; and Strachan to James Brown, 1813.04.26/1813.06.14, Firth, pp. 294-296.
97. *Kingston Gazette*, 1813.08.10.
98. Prevost to Cochrane, 1814.06.02, DH, vol. 2, p. 402.
99. Cochrane to John W. Croker, 1814.07.18, DH, vol. 2, pp. 415-416.
100. Stacey, p. 22.
101. Prevost proclamation, n.d., Stanley, p. 342.
102. Strachan to Thomas Jefferson, 1815.01.25, Hitsman, p. 211.
103. Stacey, p. 17; and Playter Diary, 1813.04.30, Firth, p. 282.
104. Auchinleck, pp. 188-189; Hitsman, p. 146; and E. A. Cruikshank, "Record of the Services of Canadian Regiments in the War of 1812: Part VI – The Canadian Voltigeurs," Canadian Military Institute *Selected Papers*, no. 10, 1900, pp. 13-14.
105. W. D. Powell to Prevost, 1813.08.01, Firth, p. 318.
106. *Kingston Gazette*, 1813.08.10.
107. Allan to Baynes, 1813.08.03, Firth, pp. 318-319.
108. John Biddulph, *The Nineteenth and Their Times* (London, 1899), p. 183; and M. L. Magill, "William Allan and the War of 1812," *Ontario History*, vol. 14, p. 140.
109. Allen to Baynes, 1813.08.03, Firth, pp. 318-319.
110. *Ibid.*, pp. 318-320.
111. Deposition of William Knot Concerning John Lyon, Nathaniel Hastings, and Timothy Wheeler, 1813.08.17, Firth, p. 320.
112. Allen to Baynes, 1813.08.03, Firth, p. 319; Firth, p. xciii; and Cruikshank, "York Militia," *passim.*
113. *Kingston Gazette*, 1813.08.10; and Biddulph, p. 183.
114. Bruyères to Freer, 1813.08.26, Firth, p. 321.
115. *Ibid.*
116. John S. Kitson Report on the Defence and the Accommodation of the Troops at York, 1813.11.22, Firth, pp. 323-324.
117. "Sketch of the ground in advance of and including York Upper Canada," 1813.11.00, NAC, NMC-22819.
118. Delivery Certificate for stone, York Garrison Account Book, 1815.07.22, p. 357, THB.
119. Kitson Report on the Defence and the Accommodation of the Troops at York, 1813.11.22, Firth, pp. 323-324.
120. Sir Gordon Drummond to Prevost, 1813.12.13, NAC, RG8, C, vol. 1221.
121. ______ Hughes to the Engineer's Office, 1814.05.28, NAC, RG8, C, vol. 388.
122. Bruyères to Prevost, 1814.01.23, Firth, p. 327.
123. Cruikshank, "York Militia," pp. 44-49.
124. Cruikshank, "Garrisons of Toronto," pp. 63-64.

125. Chauncey to the Sec. of the Navy, 1814.08.10, DH, vol. 1, pp. 126-127.
126. Thomas Ridout to T. G. Ridout, 1814.08.09, Firth, p. 333.
127. *Ibid.*; and Drummond to Prevost, 1814.08.08, DH, vol. 1, p. 125.
128. Cruikshank, "Garrisons of Toronto," p. 60.
129. John Douglas, *Medical Topography of Upper Canada*, 1819, Firth, p. 334.
130. Strachan to Owen, 1815.02.24, George W. Spragge, ed., *The John Strachan Letter Book* (Toronto, 1946), pp. 71-72.
131. *Ibid.*
132. Smelser, p. 285.
133. Elias W. Durnford Report on the State of the Fortifications, 1816.11.20, NAC, RG8, II, vol. 13.
134. Sir Frederick Philipse Robinson to Drummond, 1815.07.10, Edith G. Firth, ed., *The Town of York, 1815-1834* (Toronto, 1966), pp. 2-3.

CHAPTER THREE

1. Military Memoir of the Province of Canada by Capt. W., 1856.07.26, NAC, Record Group 8, British Military Records, hereafter RG8, II, vol. 7.
2. Report on the State of Fortifications and Military Buildings in Upper and Lower Canada, 1816.11.20, NAC, RG8, C, vol. 514.
3. Charles P. Stacey, *Canada and the British Army, 1846-1871* (London, 1936), p. 90.
4. Lecture by Desmond Morton, University of Toronto, and author of *A Military History of Canada* (Edmonton, 1985), 1989.11.03, at Fort York's Autumn Series, "The Myth of the Undefended Border: Canadian Defence from 1815-1914."
5. For a complete discussion of these issues, see, Stacey, *passim.*
6. Anonymous, "The Defence of Canada," *Blackwood's Edinburgh Magazine*, vol. 91, Feb. 1862, pp. 251-252.
7. Return of the Strength of the Garrison at York, 1829.02.13, NAC, RG8, C, vol. 434.
8. Return, Distribution, and State of the Barracks, 1825.03.24, NAC, RG8, C, vol. 577.
9. Commandant of Fort York to the Military Secretary, 1841.08.02, NAC, RG8, C, vol. 519; and Dallas Wood, "Reading Habits and Materials of the British Army Officer in Upper Canada, 1838-1841," ms. report, THB, 1986, pp. 54-56.
10. J. H. Lefroy, *Report on the Regimental and Garrison Schools of the Army, and on Military Libraries and Reading Rooms*, 1859, Carol Whitfield, *Tommy Atkins: The British Soldier in Canada, 1759-1870* (Ottawa, 1981), p. 107.
11. Sir John Colborne to ______ Couper, 1829.05.11; and Commanding Officer of the 68th Foot to the Asst. Adj.-Gen., 1834.02.07, NAC, RG8, C, vols. 580, 585.
12. Plan of "A" and "B" Barracks, 1865.05.19, THB.
13. *E.g.* Extracts from the Report of the Minutes of Inspection held on the Barracks at York, U.C. in 1826, 1827, & 1828; and Bonnycastle Memorandum, 1835.02.09, NAC, RG8, C, vols. 580, 586.
14. Proceedings of a Board of Survey held at Toronto, Upper Canada . . . for the purpose of examining into and reporting upon the State and Condition of the rooms occupied as Officers Quarters in the Garrison of Toronto, 1837.10.13, NAC, War Office Papers (hereafter WO) 55/1917.
15. *United Empire Loyalist*, 1828.02.10.
16. *The Patriot*, 1841.01.26.
17. *E.g. The York Gazette*, 1809.01.25; and *The Patriot*, 1841.01.26.

18. Fred Dreyer, "Three Years in the Toronto Garrison: The Story of the Honourable Gilbert Elliot, 1847-1850," *Ontario History*, vol. 57, *passim.*
19. *Patriot and Farmer's Monitor*, 1840.01.21.
20. Walter Henry, *Trifles from my Port-Folio*, 1843, Edith G. Firth, ed, *The Town of York, 1815-1834* (Toronto, 1966), p. 338.
21. *The Globe*, 1862.03.19; *The British Colonist*, 1847.08.31; and *The Patriot*, 1842.04.19.
22. *Colonial Advocate*, 1825.02.24.
23. Alexander Wood to Mrs. Elmsley, 1806.05.23, Edith G. Firth, ed., *The Town of York, 1793-1815* (Toronto, 1962), p. 103.
24. *The British Colonist*, 1844.08.23.
25. Excerpt from *The 93rd Sutherland Highlanders*, THB, pp. 77-78 (author, publisher, date of publication unknown).
26. *Ibid.*, p. 77.
27. *Toronto Colonist*, 1839.04.00.
28. High Bailiff's Minute Book, 1849-1854, 1849.06.08, CTA.
29. *The Mirror*, 1856.04.23.
30. Larrett Smith diary, 1843.02.17, Mary L. Smith, *Young Mr. Smith in Upper Canada* (Toronto, 1980), p. 86.
31. *The Globe*, 1861.01.03.
32. R. Byham to Sir J. Burgoyne, 1847.10.27, NAC, WO55/881.
33. Return, Distribution, and State of the Barracks, 1825.03.24, NAC, RG8, C, vol. 65.
34. Henry Powell to ______ Hillier, 1822.08.02, Firth, *1815-1834*, p. 230.
35. A. D. Thiessen, "The Founding of the Toronto Magnetic Observatory and the Canadian Meteorological Service," *Journal of the Royal Astronomical Society of Canada*, vol. 24, 1940, pp. 310-348.
36. William Lyon Mackenzie, *Independence*, n.d., Colin Read and Ronald J. Stagg, eds., *The Rebellion of 1837 in Upper Canada* (Ottawa, 1985), hereafter R&S, pp. 110-113.
37. Petition of Randal Wixon, 1838.04.10, R&S, p. 120.
38. R&S, p. xxxvi.
39. *E.g.*: Petition of Titus Root to Sir George Arthur, 1838.04.20; and Examination of Nathaniel Pearson, 1837.12.16, R&S, pp. 121-123.
40. *E.g.*: Statement of Charles Doan, 1837.12.15; and Petition of Joseph Gould to Arthur, 1838.05.04, R&S, pp. 114-117.
41. Doan Petition to Sir Francis Bond Head, 1838.03.12, R&S, p. 123.
42. Head to Lord Glenelg, 1837.12.19, R&S, p. 176; and Mary Beacock Fryer, *Volunteers and Redcoats, Rebels and Raiders: A Military History of the Rebellions in Upper Canada* (Toronto, 1987), p. 13.
43. James Barclay to ______ Baddely, 1837.11.27; and ______ Foster to Thomas Goldie, 1837.11.29, NAC, RG8, C, vol. 749.
44. William Kilbourn, *The Firebrand: William Lyon Mackenzie and the Rebellion in Upper Canada* (Toronto, 1964), p. 155.
45. R&S, pp. xxxvi-xxxviii.
46. Kilbourn, p. 155.
47. Fryer, pp. 10, 30-31; and Sir Francis Bond Head, *A Narrative* (London, 1839), pp. 330-331.
48. Pearson Examination, 1837.12.16, R&S, p. 121; and R&S, pp. xlv-xlvii.
49. Fryer, p. 32.
50. *Christian Guardian*, 1837.12.06.
51. *Ibid.*
52. Head, p. 331; and Kilbourn, p. 180.
53. Mackenzie's account of the Picket Incident, 1838.05.12, R&S, pp. 156-157.
54. *Christian Guardian*, 1837.12.06.

55. Information of George Reed, 1837.12.13, R&S, p. 168; and R&S, p. xxx.
56. Mackenzie's Account, 1838.05.12; and Statement of George Auburn, 1837.12.*c*.15, R&S, pp. 167, 171-172; and *Christian Guardian*, 1837.12.13.
57. Fryer, pp. 37-39, 41-42.
58. Head to Glenelg, 1837.12.19, R&S, pp. 175-176.
59. R&S, p. lv.
60. *Ibid.*, pp. liv-lv.
61. F. L. Bridgman to Fanny West, 1837.12.15, R&S, p. 187.
62. Fryer, p. 70.
63. ? to Goldie, 1838.05.15, NAC, RG8, C, vol. 445.
64. Militia General Order, 1838.10.23, *The Patriot*, 1838.10.26.
65. Fryer, p. 101.
66. R&S, p. xcvii; and Fryer, *passim.*
67. Fryer, *passim*; and List of Expenditures, 1837-1838, n.d., NAC, RG8, C, vol. 447.
68. Smith, p. 15; *British Colonist*, 1839.09.04; and Memorandum, 1839.11.14, NAC, RG8, C, vol. 449.
69. Diary of Alexander Cunningham Robertson, 1840.05.00, vol. 2, p. 46, MTL, Baldwin Room; and List of military expenditures, 1837-1838, n.d. NAC, RG8, C, vol. 447.
70. William Orde Mackenzie Diary, 1839.04.26, Univ. of Toronto, Fisher Library.
71. Bruce E. Cane, "The 1838 Money Vaults at Historic Fort York," ms. report, THB, 1986.
72. Commanding Officer of the Royal Engineers to the Military Sec. of the Commanding Officer of H.M. Forces in Canada, 1838.08.29; and List of Expenditures, 1837 and 1838, n.d., NAC, RG8, C, vols. 588 and 447.
73. List of Expenditures for 1837 and 1838, n.d.; and ? to ?, 1838.12.15, NAC, RG8, C, vols. 447, 446.
74. "Sketch shewing the Relative Positions of the several Barracks both Permanent and Hired Toronto – Canada," 1842.01.15, RG8, II, vol. 58.
75. ? to ?, 1838.11.04, NAC, RG8, C, vol. 466.
76. Report on military works, stores, barracks, &c, n.d.; and F. Halkett to Rowan, 1839.09.07, NAC, RG8, C, vols. 447, 591.
77. Morton, p. 79.
78. Fryer, p. 128.
79. Anonymous, "The Defence of Canada," *Blackwood's Edinburgh Magazine*, vol. 91, Feb. 1862, p. 252.
80. Sir James Carmichael Smyth Report on Defence, 1826, Firth, *1815-1834*, p. 18; and Extracts from the Report of the Minutes of Inspection held on the Barracks at York, U.C. in 1826, 1827, & 1828, n.d., NAC, RG8, C, vol. 580.
81. Smyth Report on Defence, 1826, Firth, *1815-1834*, p. 18.
82. René Laurant, *Les Ports de la Côte et du Zwin* (Brussels, 1986), p. 67.
83. Sir Frederick Philipse Robinson, 1815.00.00; and Robert Pilkington report, 1833.04.13, Firth, *1815-1834*, pp. 3-4, 33.
84. Smyth Report on Defence, 1826, Firth, *1815-1834*, p. 18.
85. "Plan of a Proposed Fort containing a casemated Fortified Barracks for 200 men proposed to be constructed at York, NAC, NMC-23140; and budget request, *c.*1826, NAC, RG8, C, vol. 428.
86. Robert Pilkington Report, 1833.04.13, Firth, *1815-1834*, p. 33.
87. Colborne to Viscount Goderich, 1833.01.23; and Pilkington Report, 1833.04.13, Firth, *1815-1834*, pp. 31-34.
88. Thomas Glegg Notebook and Sketchbook, 1841-1842, AO; and "Plan of Comparison shewing . . . the new Barrack and Work around it," 1833.12.24, THB.
89. Morton, p. 72.
90. Byham to R. W. Hay, 1835.04.15, Firth, *1815-1834*, p. xxi.

91. Firth, *1815-1834*, p. xxi.
92. "No 1, Plan of the Town and Harbour of York Upper Canada and also of the Military Reserve showing the site of the new Barracks and Work around them, as proposed to be erected near the Western Battery," 1833, Firth, *1815-1834*.
93. Glegg Notebook and Sketchbook, AO.
94. *Ibid.*
95. "Report of the Commissioners appointed to investigate certain proceedings at Toronto connected with the Election for that City laid before the House by Message from His Excellency the Governor General," 1841.08.03, United Province of Canada Legislative Assembly, *Journals*, 1841, Appendix S.
96. High Bailiff's Minute Books, 1848-1852, 1851.07.23, CTA.
97. Brereton Greenhous, *Dragoon* (Belleville, 1983), p. 164.
98. Extract from the joint report of Colonel Holloway, R.E. and Captain Boxer, R.N., 1844-1846, NAC, WO 55/887.
99. Commanding Royal Engineer in Canada to the Inspector-General of Fortifications Submitting Works of Defence for Toronto Harbour, 1854.03.25, NAC, WO 55/887.
100. *Ibid.*
101. Military Memoir of the Province of Canada, 1856.07.26, NAC, RG8, II, vol. 7.
102. NAC, RG8, vol. 1621, *passim.*
103. C. Waller to ______ Stothend?, 1862.10.31, NAC, RG8, C, vol. 1619.
104. ? to the Commanding Royal Engineer in Canada, 1862.06.17, NAC, RG8, C, vol. 1619.
105. Stacey, p. 91.
106. *Ibid.*, p. 93.
107. *Ibid.*, pp. 102-103.
108. *Ibid.*, pp. 97-100.
109. *Ibid.*, p. 100.
110. *Ibid.*, p. 170.
111. *Ibid.*, pp. 164-165.
112. John A. Macdonald, *Troublous Times in Canada: A History of the Fenian Raids of 1866 and 1870* (Toronto, 1910), pp. 33-103.
113. *Ibid.*, pp. 149-170.
114. William F. D. Jervois, *Report on the Defence of Canada & the British Naval Stations in the Atlantic* (London, 1864), *passim.*
115. William F. D. Jervois, *Report on the Defence of Canada (Made to the Provincial Government on the 10th November 1864)* (London, 1865), *passim.*
116. Jervois, 1864, p. 1.
117. *Ibid.*
118. Lecture by Prof. Desmond Morton, 1989.11.03, Fort York's Lecture Series, "The Myth of the Undefended Border: Canadian Defence from 1815-1914."
119. "Toronto, Canada West, Shewing Existing & Proposed Defences," 1865.01.00, Devon Record Office, Exeter; and Jervois, 1864, p. 9.
120. Jervois, 1864, p. 9.
121. *Ibid.*, p. 11.
122. W. Howard Russell, *Canada: its Defences, Condition, and Resources*, 2nd, ed. (Boston, 1865), p. 51.
123. Roger F. Sarty, *Coast Artillery, 1815-1914* (Bloomfield, Ont., 1988), pp. 13-14.
124. *Report on the State of the Militia of the Dominion of Canada for the Year 1870* (Ottawa, 1870), n.p.; and Thomas Wily to the Minister of Militia and Defence, 1870.09.30, NAC, RG9, Militia Records, vol. 21.
125. George F. G. Stanley, *Toil and Trouble: Military Expeditions to Red*

River (Ottawa, 1989), pp. 70-95; and D. J. Goodspeed, ed., *The Armed Forces of Canada, 1867-1967* (Ottawa: 1967), p. 12.

126. Stanley, pp. 219, 236.
127. *Ibid.*, p. 246; and Philip Goldring, "The First Contingent: The North-West Mounted Police, 1873-74," *Canadian Historic Sites: Occasional Papers in Archaeology and History*, no. 22 (Ottawa, 1979), pp. 13-14.
128. S. B. Steele, *Forty Years in Canada* (Toronto, 1915), pp. 47-49.
129. *Ibid.*
130. Robert Henry Davies, *The Canadian Militia! Its Organization and present condition* (Caledonia, Ont., 1873), p. 3.
131. Thomas Wiley Memorandum, 1871.08.01, NAC, RG9, ii, A1, vol. 32.
132. Greenhous, pp. 42-43.
133. Memorandum, 1877.*c.*05.07, Charles R. Sanderson, ed., *The Arthur Papers, Being the Papers Mainly Confidential, Private, and Demi-Official of Sir George Arthur, K.C.H.* (Toronto, 1959), vol. 3, p. 415.
134. P. Nobelton-Ross Memorandum, 1871.08.01, NAC, RG9, ii, A1, vol. 32.
135. Inspector of Artillery Memorandum, 1888.12.20, NAC, RG9, ii, A1, vol. 221.
136. Roger Sarty, "Canadian Maritime Defence, 1892-1914," ms. report, Directorate of History, Dept. of National Defence, n.d. For a good discussion of late nineteenth and early twentieth century defensive preparations, see: Stephen J. Harris, *Canadian Brass: The Making of a Professional Army, 1860-1939* (Toronto, 1988), *passim.*
137. Harris, p. 170.
138. Aldona Sendzikas, "The Last Bastion: The Story of Stanley Barracks," M.A. Thesis, Univ. of Toronto, 1990, pp. 92-101.
139. Commissioner of Parks to H. R. Alley, 1943.05.15; Commissioner of Parks Memorandum, 1943.03.18, and general Parks Dept. Records for the war years, CTA.
140. Catherine Groth Sparrow, "Little Norway – Muskoka – Vesle Skaugum: Training Centers of the Royal Norwegian Air Force in Canada," *American-Scandinavian Review*, Sept. 1942, pp. 204-215.

CHAPTER FOUR

1. ______ McMurrich to the Dept. of Militia and Defence, 1889.01.26, NAC, Record Group 9, Militia Records, hereafter RG9, ii, A1, vol. 221.
2. Albert Paul to the Minister of Militia and Defence, 1898.07.18, NAC, RG9, ii, A1, vol. 300.
3. Various correspondence between the Dept. of Militia and Defence and the Canadian Club of Toronto, 1899, NAC, RG9, ii, A1, vol. 315.
4. Gerald Killan, *Preserving Ontario's Heritage: A History of the Ontario Historical Society* (Ottawa, 1976), pp. 127-129.
5. *Annual Report of the Ontario Historical Society 1909*, Killan, p. 129.
6. *Ibid.*, p. 130.
7. "Plan of the Proposed Improvements on part of the Ordnance Reserve Toronto," *c.*1856, NAC, NMC-19783; Thomas Wiley Memorandum, 1871.08.01, NAC, RG9, ii, A1, vol. 32; Memorandum, 1890.00.00, NAC, RG9, ii, A1, vol. 238, file A10, 155-A10-164; Killan, pp. 152-153; and Thomas Tait to C. E. Panet, 1893.04.18, NAC, RG9, ii, A1, vol. 267, A12-701.
8. D. A. Macdonald to the Minister of Militia and Defence, 1903.06.08, AO, Fort York Collection.
9. Ordnance Land Sale Grant to the Corporation of the City of Toronto, 1909.05.17, THB.

10. Jean Earle Geeson to the *Globe*, 1905.10.04; and "The Old Fort at Toronto Restored," map produced by the Ontario Historical Society, 1909.01.12, MTL, Ms-S-84.
11. *Ibid.*, p. 138.
12. *Ibid.*, pp. 139-161; and OHS, *Memorandum to accompany the Plans of the Restoration of Old Fort York* (Toronto, 1909), p. 3.
13. Killan, p. 150.
14. *Ibid.*, pp. 145-147.
15. *Ibid.*, pp. 151-152.
16. *Evening News*, 1905.10.09.
17. Killan, pp. 136, 160-161; and photograph of the cookhouse/officers' quarters area, 1926, NAC, PA-87473.
18. Commissioner of Parks to the Mayor and Board of Control of the Corp. of the City of Toronto, 1908.09.22, CTA, RG12, A, Box 6, Dept. of Parks Records.
19. Commissioner of Parks to H. R. Alley, 1943.05.15, CTA, Parks Dept. Records.
20. Killan, p. 206.
21. Plan of the Fort at York Upper Canada shewing its state in March 1816, by Jean-Baptiste Duberger 1816.02.16 and signed by Gustavus Nicolls, 1816.06.14, NAC, NMC-23139. This map commonly is known as the "Nicolls' Plan."
22. *The Globe*, 1934.05.24-25.
23. Shirley McManus, "History of the Toronto Civic Historical Committee, 1949-1960 and the Toronto Historical Board, 1960-1985" (ms. report, THB, 1986), pp. 4-5.
24. John Scott, "Fort York," *The York Pioneer*, vol. 54, 1959, pp. 2-6.
25. *Ibid.*, pp. 5-6.
26. Killan, pp. 242-243.
27. Consultant's Report prepared by Dillon Consulting Engineers on the Front Street Extension for the Municipality of Metropolitan Toronto (Toronto, 1986), Metro Toronto Transportation Dept.

SELECT BIBLIOGRAPHY

This catalogue serves as a comprehensive historical and museological bibliography on Fort York up to the beginning of 1993 as well as a listing of material containing significant sections about the fort or the colonial military history of Toronto. Items about Fort York marked with an asterisk are recommended because of the quantity or quality of information they contain. A perusal of the endnotes will provide more sources, including manuscript material. As well as the works listed here, most general histories of the War of 1812 and the Rebellion of 1837 have sections on Fort York or the military history of early Toronto. The regimental histories of units stationed at Fort York, biographies of principal players in York's history (such as John Strachan), and histories of Toronto often have information about Toronto's early military history. However, general histories, in addition to their brevity, often are inaccurate.

Other sources of information are the various pamphlets and other similar publications produced by the city agencies responsible for the fort over the years, especially the Toronto Historical Board. In 1991, the THB began a newsletter, *Explore Historic Toronto,* which contains articles and notices about Fort York of historical and museological interest.

______. "Recollections of a Sailor," *Military and Naval Magazine of the United States*, vol. 3, 1834.

______. "Sir Roger Hale Sheaffe and the defence of York," *Anglo-American Magazine*, vol. 3, 1853. This magazine published a detailed history of the War of 1812 (including documents). The history was then reprinted in book form as: Auchinleck, Gilbert. *A History of the War between Great Britain and the United States during the Years 1812, 1813 & 1814*. Toronto: Maclear and Company, 1855; reprinted London: Arms and Armour Press, 1972.

______. "Description of the Attack and Occupation of York," Women's Canadian Historical Society of Toronto *Transactions*, no. 5, 1905.

______. "Fort York Wins a Modern Battle," *Ontario History*, vol. 51, 1959. Re the fight to save Fort York from being moved for the Gardiner Expressway.

______. "The Capture of York," *The York Pioneer*, vol. 62, 1967.

Alley, Herbert Ruttan. *Fort York, Toronto: An Historical Sketch*. Toronto: Toronto Civic Historical Committee, 1954.

Andre, John. *Infant Toronto as Simcoe's Folly*. Toronto: Centennial Press, 1971. This is a controversial work disputing Simcoe's importance in the establishment of York and suggests that William Berczy deserves much of the credit.

*Benn, Carl. *The Battle of York*. Belleville, Ont.: Mika, 1984.

*______. "The Military Context of the Founding of Toronto," *Ontario History*, vol. 81, 1989.

______. "Free-Standing Bombproof Gunpowder Magazines of the War of 1812 Period in Upper Canada." *Arms Collecting*, vol. 29, 1991. Contains material about the two Fort York magazines.

______. "Research at Fort York Expands Images of 19th Century Military Life," Toronto Historical Board, *Explore Historic Toronto*, no. 1, Sept. 1991.

______. "Toronto's Forgotten Fort" [Stanley Barracks], Toronto Historical Board, *Explore Historic Toronto*, no. 2, Apr. 1992.

[______ *et al.*]. *Fort York: A Master Plan for Redevelopment*. Toronto: THB, 1990.

*Bradford, Robert D. *Historic Forts of Ontario*. Belleville, Ont.: Mika, 1988. Chapter 5 is about Fort York.

Brandis, Marianne. *Fire Ship*. Erin, Ont.: Porcupine Press, 1992. A children's novel focused on the Battle of York.

Brown, Donald A. "The 1987 Fort York Archaeology Programme – a Preliminary Assessment," *Profile* (newsletter of the Toronto Chapter of the Ontario Archaeological Society), Jan.-Feb. 1987.

Bull, Stewart H. *Queen's York Rangers*. Erin, Ont.: Boston Mills Press, 1984.

______. "The Queen's Rangers in the Rebellion of 1837," *The York Pioneer*, vol. 82, 1987.

Burns, Robert. "'Queer doings': Attitudes towards homosexuality in 19th century Canada," *Our Image: The Body Politic Review*, no. 6, December-January 1976-1977. This article explores the controversy surrounding a homosexual scandal in Upper Canada in the late 1830s which involved a number of soldiers from Fort York.

Cain, Bruce E. "Dr. Shortt, M.D.," *Journal of the Society for Army Historical Research*, vol. 66, 1988. A brief article on a portrait of a military surgeon in the Fort York collection. Short served at Fort York in the second quarter of the nineteenth century.

Cain, Emily. *Ghost Ships: Hamilton and Scourge: Historical Treasures from the War of 1812*. Toronto: Musson, 1983. Tells the story of shipbuilding on Lake Ontario during the War of 1812 era with special emphasis on two schooners, the USS *Hamilton* and the USS *Scourge*, which participated in the Battle of York but which sank in an action near Burlington later in 1813.

*Chewett, William *et al.* "The Capture of York," *The York Pioneer*, vol. 62, 1967. This is one of the letters Chewett and his supporters wrote to condemn Sheaffe's actions in the Battle of York and cover up their own incompetence.

Compton-Smith, C. *The Capture of York; a Collection of Documents and Records together with Factual Reports, dealing with events of the Day*. Toronto: McGraw-Hill, 1968.

Craig, Hamilton. "The Loyal and Patriotic Society of Upper Canada and its Still-Born Child – The Upper Canada Preserved Medal," *Ontario History*, vol. 52, 1960. Covers the society that was founded and centred in York during the War of 1812 to provide support and recognition to militiamen and their families.

Crawford, Michael, and Kenneth Armstrong, comps. *The Fenians* (Jackdaw No. 21). Toronto: Clarke, Irwin & Company, 1970. This is a collection of documents and illustrations relating to the Fenian Raids produced mainly for use in the schools. Much of the material was drawn from the Fort York collection.

*Cruikshank, Ernest A., ed. *Documentary History of the Campaign on the Niagara Frontier*, 9 vols. Niagara and Welland: Niagara Historical Society, 1902-1908. Vols. 4 and 5 have large amounts of information about the Battle of York although references to York are found throughout the series.

*______. "Record of the Services of Canadian Regiments in the War of 1812: Part XIII. – The York Militia," Canadian Military Institute *Selected Papers*, no. 16, 1908.

*______, ed. *The Correspondence of Lieut. Governor John Graves Simcoe, with Allied Documents Relating to His Administration of the Government of Upper Canada*, 5 vols. Toronto: Ontario Historical Society, 1923-1931.

______. ed. *The Correspondence of the Honourable Peter Russell with Allied Documents relating to his Administration of the Government of Upper Canada during the Official Term of Lieut.-Governor J. G. Simcoe while on Leave of Absence*, 3 vols. Toronto: Ontario Historical Society, 1932-1936. This work is not as rich in Fort York data as the Simcoe Papers, but does contain a modest amount of material on the fort after Simcoe's departure and on the Mississauga Crisis.

*______. "The Garrisons of Toronto and York, 1750-1815," *Canadian Military Institute Papers* (1934-1935).

Cumberland, Barlow. *The Battle of York*. Toronto: William Briggs, 1913.

Cummins, J. F. "Notes on the Military History of Toronto," *Canadian Defence Quarterly*, vol. 5, 1927-1928.

Douglas, John. *Medical Topography of Upper Canada*. Canton, Maine: Science History Publications, 1985. Reprint of the 1819 edition. Douglas served at York during part of the War of 1812.

*Dreyer, Fred. "Three Years in the Toronto Garrison: The Story of the Honourable Gilbert Elliot, 1847-1850," *Ontario History*, vol. 57, 1965. Good social history on an officer's life in Toronto.

Edgar, Matilda. "The Explosion of the Magazine at York, April 27, 1813," Women's Canadian Historical Society of Toronto *Transactions*, vol. 10, 1912.

Eustis, Abraham. "The Capture of York," Massachusetts Historical Society *Proceedings*, vol. 11, 1869-1871.

*Finan, P. "An Onlooker's View," John Gellner, ed., *Recollections of the War of 1812*. Toronto: Baxter, 1964. Finan was a boy who witnessed the Battle of York.

*Firth, Edith G., ed. *The Town of York, 1793-1815: A Collection of Documents of Early Toronto*. Toronto: Champlain Society, 1962.

______, ed. *The Town of York, 1815-1834: A Further Collection of Documents of Early Toronto*. Toronto: Champlain Society, 1966.

Fitzgibbon, Mary Agnes. "Deeds Speak," Women's Canadian Historical Society of Toronto *Transactions*, no. 1, 1896. An interesting account of the colours of the 3rd Regiment of York Militia during the War of 1812.

*Fryer, Mary Beacock. *Volunteers and Redcoats, Rebels and Raiders: A Military History of the Rebellions in Upper Canada*. Toronto and Oxford: Dundurn Press, 1987.

Geeson, Jean E. *The Old Fort at Toronto, 1793-1906*. Toronto: William Briggs, 1906.

Gerrard, Richard. "Beyond Crossmends: Stratigraphic Analysis and the Content of Historic Artifact Assemblages on Urban Sites," E. Harris and M. Brown, eds., *The Practices of Archaeological Stratigraphy.* London: Academic Press, 1990. A technical article based on material uncovered during archaeological work at Fort York in 1987.

Guillet, Edwin C. *Early Life in Upper Canada.* Toronto: University of Toronto Press, 1933. This book contains several chapters dealing with the founding of Toronto, the Battle of York, the Rebellion of 1837, and the Fenian Raids. It is a useful book for understanding the state of popular history related to Fort York at the time the fort was restored as a historic site.

Hannon, Leslie F. *Forts of Canada.* Toronto: McClelland and Stewart, 1969. Chapter 5 and the Epilogue contain material about Fort York.

Hathaway, Ernest J. "The Story of the Old Fort at Toronto," *Ontario History,* vol. 25, 1929. Also reprinted in booklet form, Toronto: MacMillan, 1934.

Hayes, John F. *Treason at York.* Vancouver: Copp Clark, n.d., (*c.*1950). A children's novel about York during the War of 1812.

______. *Rebels Ride at Night.* Vancouver: Copp Clark, 1953. A children's novel about Toronto during the Rebellion of 1837.

*Head, Francis Bond. *A Narrative* [of the Rebellion of 1837]. London: John Murray, 1839.

Historical, Military and Patriotic Societies. *Memorandum to accompany the Plans of the Restoration of Old Fort York.* Toronto: Ontario Historical Society, 1909.

Hollon, W. E. "Zebulon Montgomery Pike and the York Campaign, 1813," *New York History,* vol. 30, 1949. While the description of the Battle of York is inaccurate, this article is interesting in its portrayal of Pike and the American army in the months leading up to the attack.

*Humphries, Charles. "The Capture of York," *Ontario History,* vol. 51, 1959. (Reprinted in Morris Zaslow, ed., *The Defended Border: Upper Canada and the War of 1812,* Toronto: Macmillan, 1964.)

Hunter, A. F. "The Parts Borne by Fort Rouille and Fort York in the Establishment of Toronto," *Ontario History,* vol. 25, 1929.

Ibbitson, John. *1812: Jeremy and the General.* Don Mills: Maxwell Macmillan, 1991. A children's novel on the War of 1812 with a Toronto area focus.

Jarvis, Murray G. "Details of the Capture of York, April 27, 1813," Women's Canadian Historical Society of Toronto *Transactions,* vol. 5, 1905.

Johnson, J. K. "The Social Composition of the Toronto Bank Guards, 1837-1838," *Ontario History,* vol. 64, 1972.

*Johnson, Leo A. "The Mississauga-Lake Ontario Land Surrender of 1805," *Ontario History,* vol. 83, 1990. An excellent article on the Mississauga crisis of the 1790s.

Kellett, Anthony, "Messes and Canteens in Canada from their Origins to 1914," *Military Collector & Historian,* vol. 31, 1979. Contains photographs and other references to messes and canteens in the Toronto garrison.

Kerr, W. B. "The Occupation of York," *Canadian Historical Review,* vol. 5, 1924.

Killan, Gerald. "The First Old Fort York Preservation Movement, 1905-1909: An Episode in the History of the Ontario Historical Society," *Ontario History,* vol. 64, 1972.

______. "The York Pioneers and the First Old Fort York Preservation Movement, 1905-1909," *The York Pioneer,* vol. 68, 1973.

*______. *Preserving Ontario's Heritage: A History of the Ontario Historical Society.* Toronto: Ontario Historical Society, 1976. Chapter 5 contains a detailed account of the fight to preserve Fort York from destruction in the first decades of the twentieth century.

Lancaster, Bruce. *Bright the Wanderer.* Boston: Little, Brown and Company, 1942. A novel about the Rebellion of 1837 with a strong Toronto focus.

Lucas, Fiona. "Uncovering an 1826 Hearth and Oven: Fort York Gets a New Old Kitchen," *Food History News,* vol. 4, Spring 1993.

[______]. "Recipes from the Mess Establishment, Officers' Brick Barracks at Fort York," Toronto Historical Board, *Explore Historic Toronto,* no. 1, Sept. 1991.

[______]. "Recipes from the Mess Establishment, Officers' Brick Barracks at Fort York," Toronto Historical Board, *Explore Historic Toronto,* no. 2, Apr. 1992.

[______]. "Recipes from the Mess Establishment, Officers' Brick Barracks at Fort York," Toronto Historical Board, *Explore Historic Toronto,* no. 3, Nov. 1992.

*Mackenzie, William Lyon. *Mackenzie's Own Narrative of the Late Rebellion with Illustrations and Notes, Critical and Explanatory: Exhibiting the Only True Account of What Took Place at the Memorable Siege of Toronto in the Month of December 1837.* Ottawa: Golden Dog Press, 1980. Reprint of Mackenzie's narrative published in 1838.

*Macleod, Malcolm. "Fortress Ontario or Forlorn Hope? Simcoe and the Defence of Upper Canada," *Canadian Historical Review,* vol. 53, 1972.

Magill, M. L. "William Allan and the War of 1812," *Ontario History,* vol. 64, 1972. Allan was the second-in-command of the York Militia during the Battle of York.

McInnis, John A. "Fort York, 1813-1963," *The York Pioneer,* vol. 58, 1963.

Middleton, Jessie E. "York, Canada, in the War of 1812," *Americana,* vol. 18, 1924.

Millman, T. R., ed. "Roger Hale Sheaffe and the defence of York, April 27, 1813," *Canadian Church Historical Society Journal,* vol. 5, 1963.

Morton, Desmond. "Sir William Otter and the Internment Operations in Canada during the First World War," *Canadian Historical Review,* vol. 55, 1974. Discusses the use of Stanley Barracks for the internment of enemy aliens.

Murray, John M., ed. "A Recovered Letter: W. W. Baldwin to C. B. Wyatt, 6th April 1813," *Ontario History,* vol. 35, 1943.

*Myers, Ned. *Ned Myers; or, A Life Before the Mast.* Edited by James Fenimore Cooper. Annapolis: Naval Institute Press, 1989. Reprint of the 1843 edition. Myers was a rating on the American Lake Ontario squadron and participated in the Battle of York.

Newlands, David L. "The Fort York Guardhouse," Royal Ontario Museum *Archaeological Newsletter,* New Series, no. 118, 1975.

______. "The Fort York Excavations – Clay Tobacco Pipe Fragments," *The York Pioneer,* vol. 74, 1979.

Old Fort York Advisory Committee. *Fort York, Toronto, Ontario.* Toronto: OFYAC, 1936[?].

Quaife, Milo M. *The Yankees Capture York.* Detroit: Wayne State University, 1955. This pamphlet attempts to prove that the Americans were not responsible for the burning of the Parliament Buildings in York. Few historians accept Quaife's thesis.

*Read, Colin, and Ronald J. Stagg, eds. *The Rebellion of 1837 in Upper Canada: A Collection of Documents.* Ottawa: Champlain Society, 1985.

*Riddell, William Renwick. *The Life of John Graves Simcoe, First Lieutenant-Governor of the Province of Upper Canada, 1792-96.* Toronto: McClelland & Stewart, 1926.

Scott, John. "Fort York," *The York Pioneer,* vol. 54, 1959. An article about the expressway fight of the 1950s.

Sendzikas, Aldona. "The Last Bastion: The Story of Stanley Barracks," M.A. Thesis, University of Toronto, 1990.

Sheppard, George. "'Deeds Speak': Militiamen, Medals, and the Invented Traditions of 1812," *Ontario History,* vol. 83, 1990. An interesting, if exaggerated, condemnation of the Loyal and Patriotic Society and the performance of the Upper Canadian militia during the War of 1812, particularly in York.

*Simcoe, Elizabeth. *The Diary of Mrs. John Graves Simcoe, Wife of the First Lieutenant-Governor of the Province of Upper Canada, 1792-1796.* Edited by John Ross Robertson. Toronto: William Briggs, 1911.

Spragge, George W., ed. "A Letter from Government House, Toronto, December 1837," *Ontario History,* vol. 51, 1959. An interesting eyewitness account of the Rebellion from the viewpoint of an employee of the lieutenant-governor.

*Stacey, Charles P. *The Battle of Little York.* Toronto: THB, 1971. (Reprint of an article in the *Globe Magazine,* 1963.)

Stuart, Jacqueline. "The Old Military Burial Ground Toronto," *The York Pioneer,* vol. 78, 1983.

Summers, John. *Dessert Recipes From the Mess Establishment, Officers' Brick Barracks, Historic Fort York.* Toronto: THB, 1987.

______. "Developing a Souvenir with Footnotes, or, Why Historical Accuracy Doesn't Have to Go Out the Window When Visitors Come In the Door," Interpretation and Tourism: A National Conference on Heritage Interpretation, *Proceedings.* A museological paper based on the development of souvenir items at Fort York with value in interpreting history.

______. "Beyond Brown Bread and Oatmeal Cookies: New Directions for Historic Kitchens," *Material History Bulletin,* Spring 1988. An article on new approaches to interpreting historic kitchens based on the development of new programming in the fort's officers' mess kitchen.

______. "Research Worksheets for Historic Food," *Museum Quarterly,* Spring 1990. As with the above articles by John Summers, this is based on research undertaken in Fort York's domestic interpretation.

Thiessen, A. D. "The Founding of the Toronto Magnetic Observatory and the Canadian Meteorological Service," *Journal of the Royal Astronomical Society of Canada,* vol. 24, 1940. Contains detail about the observatory when it was located at the Bathurst Street Barracks.

*Waters, George, and Donald Feather. *Fort York.* Toronto: Ginn and Company, 1972. A good little book written mainly for younger readers.

Webb, Catherine. "1987 Fort York Archaeology Project," *Annual Archaeological Report of the Ontario Heritage Foundation,* vol. 1, 1990.

______. "1988 Fort York Archaeology Project," *Annual Archaeological Report of the Ontario Heritage Foundation,* vol. 1, 1990.

______. "1989 Fort York Archaeology Project," *Annual Archaeological Report of the Ontario Heritage Foundation,* vol. 1, 1990.

______. "1990 Fort York Archaeology Project," *Annual Archaeological Report of the Ontario Heritage Foundation,* vol. 2, 1991.

Webster, Donald Blake. "The Queen's Rangers (1st American Regiment)," *Military Collector & Historian,* vol. 41, 1989.

Young, Richard J. "Blockhouses of Canada, 1749-1841," *Occasional Papers in Archaeology and History,* no. 23. Ottawa: Parks Canada, 1980. Includes material on the Toronto blockhouses.

INDEX

Note: Page numbers in italics refer to the illustrations and the associated captions on the indicated pages.

Carl Benn was born, raised and educated in Toronto. He has worked in the heritage field for about twenty years and presently is the Curator of Military and Marine History for the Toronto Historical Board. He also teaches on a part-time basis at the University of Toronto and has published a large number of historical and museological articles. His next book, nearing completion, is a study of the Iroquois in the War of 1812.